The Ancestry and Descendants

of

John Grosvenor

of

Roxbury, Massachusetts

by

Richard Grosvenor

HERITAGE BOOKS
2010

HERITAGE BOOKS

AN IMPRINT OF HERITAGE BOOKS, INC.

Books, CDs, and more—Worldwide

For our listing of thousands of titles see our website
at
www.HeritageBooks.com

Published 2010 by
HERITAGE BOOKS, INC.
Publishing Division
100 Railroad Ave. #104
Westminster, Maryland 21157

International Standard Book Numbers
Paperbound: 978-0-7884-0762-8
Clothbound: 978-0-7884-8375-2

This book is dedicated
to my wife,
Anna,
who prepared it for
publication
and to our daughter,
Dorothy,
who proof read it.

G

TABLE OF CONTENTS

ANCESTRY OF JOHN GROSVENOR

Prior to 1918, when Daniel Kent published his research, Grosvenor family tradition held that John GROSVENOR, the first Grosvenor to come to America, was descended from the prominent Grosvenor family of Chester, England. Kent examined the coat of arms on John's tomb at Roxbury, Massachusetts (now a part of Boston) and went to England to find John's ancestry.

At the College of Arms in London, Kent found a pedigree of the Grosvenor family that had been drawn up by John's eldest brother Leicester in 1663. The pedigree showed John's descent from the Grosvenors of Bridgnorth. Kent also discovered the wills of John's father and grandfather and parish records at St. Leonard's church which confirmed the line of the pedigree.

Kent was not able to find the name of John's great grandfather. He left it blank on his genealogy while listing the names of his children. He thought that John's great grandfather might be William who died at Bridgnorth in 1589.

In Burke's "American Families with British Ancestry, 1939" John's great grandfather is listed as Richard GROSVENOR who died prior to 1595. Burke then lists eleven generations of Grosvenors back to Adam de GRAVENOR who lived during the reign of Edward I (1272-1307). Burke's Grosvenor genealogy was written by Joseph Morriss of Shrewsbury, Shropshire, who does not give his sources. I can find out very little about his eleven generations. The complete ancestry is now as follows:

Adam de GRAVENOR of Claverly, Salop, lived in the time of Edward I (r.1272-1307). He and his wife Margery were parents of William.

William de GRAVENOR of Claverly is mentioned in historical documents in 1324, 1331 and 1333. He had a son Richard.

Richard de GRAVENOR of Claverly, mentioned in 1376, lived during the time of Richard II (r.1377-1399). He married Agnes and left a son Richard.

Richard GRAVENOR of High Gravenor, Claverly, married Alice (d.1412). They had a son Thomas.

Thomas GRAVENOR, who died before his mother, left three sons including Henry.

Henry GRAVENOR of Heathlon died in 1435 leaving his wife Edith and sons John and Humphrey.

John GRAVENOR, the eldest son of Henry, lived at High Gravenor and died in 1496. He and his wife Agnes had sons Thomas, William, Richard and John.

John GRAVENOR of Whitmore and Bobbington, Salop, left a son William.

William GROSVENOR of Whitmore left a son Roland.

Roland GROSVENOR lived at Heathton and Whitmore. He died in 1522 at his home in Bridgnorth leaving, by his wife Eleanor, a son William.

> Roland served as Shropshire County Clerk from 1496-1507. He was bailiff of Bridgnorth ten times between 1495 and 1523 and sat for Parliaments of 1487, 1497 and 1504. It is possible that there were two Roland GROSVENORS. ("A History of Shropshire" Vol. 3)

William GROSVENOR was buried in the parish of St. Leonard, Bridgnorth on 30 Oct. 1589. His wife Margaret was buried there on 5 Oct 1583. They left a son Richard.

Richard GROSVNOR b. 1537, married Martha BLOUNT at Vores in 1566. They had 3 children. Richard died before 1595.
1. William GROSVENOR
2. Roger GROSVENOR of Coventry Co., Warwick
3. Joyce GROSVENOR
Roger and Joyce were both living in 1599 when they were mentioned in the will of their brother William.

William GROSVENOR married Ursula BLOUNT on 16 Nov. 1590. William's messuage was named "The Friars." The name may have been derived from the priory of the Grey Friars that existed in Bridgnorth before the dissolution of the monasteries in the reign of Henry VIII. Children of William and Ursula were William, bapt. 18 Dec 1593 and Margaret (or Margery) bapt. 16 May 1596. She married Richard PHILLIPS on 2 June 1630 and later married John HORD.

William's Will, dated 28 Dec 1599, included the following: Margery was to receive the income from the great meadow above "The Fryer" for a period of six years to serve as a marriage good. William, his sonne and heire, would receive his table boards upon a frame.

Joice GRAUENOR, his sister, shall receive the tenement on Lesley street for a yearlie payment of 3s 4d to his heires. His wife Ursula was entrusted with bringing up his two children. She should "bring up his sonne to be a scholler if he prove apt, if not to learn to write and read and set him to some good occupation." His wife was also to receive the income from his estate until William was of age and then have a third part of his estate as "her jointure which the law doth appoint." "All my landes, tenements, and hereditments I give to my sonne William GRAVENOR." "All my wearing apparrell I give to Roger GRAVENOR of Coventry, being my brother."

2

William GROSVENOR died on 17 Jan 1599/1600 and was buried in the parish of St. Leonard, Bridgnorth. Ursula married John DAVIES on 4 June 1600.

William, the son of William, married Susanna PASTON in about 1625. She was the daughter of Rev. George PASTON, Rector of Drayton-Basset Co., Stafford. William was the church Warden of St. Leonard's Church in 1635 and was a Royalist in the Civil War. His church had been founded in the tenth or 11th century and was constructed mainly in the 13th century style with a fine timbered roof and stained glass windows. The nave was remarkable for its 91 foot width which was not exceeded by any parish church in England and by only three cathedrals.

The post to which William was appointed by the church Vestry had many duties including care of the parish property and income. He supervised the education and relief of the poor and helped the pastor record all baptisms, marriages and deaths in the church record. Once a year the record was sent to the Bishop. William died on 21 June 1652 and Susanna died on 20 June 1667.

The children of William and Susanna were:
1. Susanna GROSVENOR b. c.1626
2. Leicester GROSVENOR b. c.1627, d. 14 May 1690, m. Eleanor EASTWICKE c.1652. Their children were Leicester, Christopher, Eleanor, Susanna, William and Eastwicke. Leicester presented a pedigree of his family to the College of Arms in London to prove descent from the Grosvenors of Chester. "Nothing was done therein."
3. Mary GROSVENOR b. c.1631 m. Edward HARRISON
4. Lettice GROSVENOR b. c.1630 m. Thomas LEVINGE, d. 1690
5. Gerald GROSVENOR b. c.1631 d. at Bridgnorth 27 June 1671
6. Grace GROSVENOR b. c.1632 m. Daniel Billingsley of Bridgnorth after 27 May 1652.
7. William GROSVENOR b. 17 Apr. 1634 at Bridgnorth, buried there on Feb. 3, 1672/3.
8. Jane GROSVENOR b. 26 July 1636 at Bridgnorth m. Francis BAYLEY of Bridgnorth after 27 May 1652.
9. John GROSVENOR b. 2 Jan 1640/41 at Bridgnorth.

DESCENDANTS OF JOHN GROSVENOR

FIRST GENERATION

1   John GROSVENOR b. 2 Jan 1640/1641 at Bridgnorth, Shropshire,
     ENG; d. 27 Sep 1691 at Roxbury, MA; bur. at Roxbury, MA.
          John GROSVENOR was born to William GROSVENOR and Susanna
     PASTON of Bridgnorth, Shropshire Co., England. When John was
     12 his father died and, according to the custom of
     primogeniture, John's eldest brother inherited his father's
     estate. Bridgnorth was famous for its tanneries and the fine
     leather that they produced and John became a tanner.
          John emigrated to America in about 1670 and lived at
     Roxbury, a suburb of Boston.   He married Esther CLARKE,
     daughter of Hugh and Elizabeth CLARKE, in 1672 and Hugh gave
     him two pieces of land. John constructed his house at Tremont
     and Parker streets in Roxbury. This land contained four acres
     of orchard and pasture. He built his tan house and tan yard
     upon the small piece of land. He was the first tanner in
     Roxbury and in 1678 the town granted him land at the bridge
     and the mill for liming leather for a fee. It was not to be
     sold but could be forfeited if it damaged water for men or for
     cattle.
          John was elected Town Constable, a position of
     importance. He arrested common criminals, Sabbath breakers,
     and drunks. He served warrants and served writs to jurors to
     ensure their presence in court. He also collected taxes that
     were levied by the General Assembly. These duties made his
     position highly unpopular and many men paid fines rather than
     serve.
          John was one of the dozen purchasers of the Mashomoquet
     grant of 15,100 acres in Connecticut. The purchase was made
     on 1 May 1686 from Major James FITCH but the survey and
     division of the land was not made until after John's death.
     In 1694 John's widow went to Windham County to receive his 502
     acres of land. (Kent)
          John GROSVENOR m. Esther CLARKE abt 1672 at Roxbury, CT.
     Esther, dau. of Hugh CLARKE and Elizabeth (____), b. abt 1651;
     d. 15 Jun 1738 at Pomfret, Windham Co., CT.
          Esther CLARKE GROSVENOR was appointed administrator of
     her husband's estate in Feb 1691/2. In 1695 she sold John's
     land in Roxbury and bought land at Muddy River (Brookline)
     Massachusetts. On 15 April 1701 she sold the property at
     Muddy River and moved to Pomfret to live on the land that had
     been purchased by John. Her sons aided in bringing the land
     under cultivation and Esther lived there for the rest of her
     life. She was a woman of great courage and energy and was
     held in highest esteem by the settlers of Pomfret. She was
     known for her skill in tending the sick. (Bowen) (Kent)

FIRST GENERATION

Children:

```
+   2 M   i    Rev. William GROSVENOR
    3 M   ii   John GROSVENOR Jr.  b. 6 Jun 1675 at Roxbury, MA;
                d. 22 Jul 1710 at Brookfield, MA.
                John, a farmer of Brookline and Brookfield MA, came
                to Brookfield in 1701.  At this time his mother
                moved to Pomfret.  John was killed by Indians while
                working in his hay field.  (Bowen)
                    John GROSVENOR Jr. m. Sarah HAYWARD 27 Jan
                1709 at Concord, MA.  Sarah, dau. of John HAYWARD
                and Anna (_____), b. 16 Jun 1689.
+   4 M   iii  Leicester GROSVENOR.
    5 F   iv   Susanna GROSVENOR b. 9 Feb 1680/1681 at Roxbury, CT.
                She m. Joseph SHAW 26 Mar 1703 at Woodstock, CT.
                Joseph, son of John SHAW, c. 22 Apr 1683.
    6 U   v    Child STILLBORN b. 21 Apr 1683.
+   7 M   vi   Ebenezer GROSVENOR
+   8 M   vii  Thomas GROSVENOR
    9 M   viii Joseph GROSVENOR  b. 1 Sep 1689 Pomfret, CT; d. 20
                Jun 1738.
```

SECOND GENERATION

2   Rev. William GROSVENOR, b. 8 Jan 1672/1673, Roxbury, MA; d.
     1733. William graduated from Harvard in 1693.
         He was a minister at Brookfield, Massachusetts, from 1705
     to 1708. Because of Indian attacks the town was unable to
     support a minister after 1708 and William went to a new church
     in Charleston, South Carolina. (Bowen)
         Rev. William GROSVENOR m. Sarah (_____).

   Children:
```
    10 F  i    Susanna GROSVENOR.
    11 F  ii   Esther GROSVENOR.
    12 F  iii  Elizabeth GROSVENOR.
```

4   Leicester GROSVENOR, b. 1676, Roxbury, MA; d. 8 Sep 1759,
     Pomfret, Windham Co., CT.
         Leicester was an ensign in the military company at
     Pomfret and was later Captain. He was elected 19 times to the
     office of town selectman. He was a member of the committee to
     select the site of the first church at Pomfret and served on
     the building committee. He also helped to establish a library
     for the propagation of useful and Christian knowledge.
     (Bowen)
         Leicester GROSVENOR m. (1) Mary HUBBARD 16 Jan 1711/1712,
     Woodstock, CT. Mary, dau. of John HUBBARD and Rebecca (_____),
     b. 1687; d. 14 May 1724, Pomfret, CT.

SECOND GENERATION

Children:
```
    13 F  i    Esther GROSVENOR, b. 27 Oct 1712; d. 10 Apr 1795,
                          Sturbridge, MA.     She  m.  John
                          TARBELL. John, b. abt 1710; d. abt
                          1804.
    14 F  ii   Jerusha GROSVENOR, b. 15 Apr 1714; d. 3 May 1739.
    15 F  iii  Mary GROSVENOR, b. 28 Dec 1715; d. 23 May 1758,
               Woodstock, CT.
               She m. Ebenezer PAINE, Ebenezer, b. 15 Oct 1711,
               Woodstock, CT; d. 29 Mar 1789, Woodstock, CT.
    16 F  iv   Anna GROSVENOR, b. 27 May 1719.
               She m. Josiah WHEELER 14 Dec 1735, Pomfret, CT.
    17 F  v    Zerviah GROSVENOR, b. 24 Jun 1721, Pomfret, Windham
               Co., CT; d. 12 Dec 1803, Pomfret, CT.  She m.
               Samuel LYON 20 Oct 1748.  Samuel, son of Abiel LYON
               and Judith FARRINGTON, b. 3 Jan 1720, Pomfret, CT;
               d. 23 Aug 1774, Pomfret, CT.
               Child: Mary Lyon  (Bowen)
    18 F  vi   Sarah GROSVENOR, b. 1 Jun 1723, Pomfret, Windham
               Co., CT; d. 14 Sep 1742.
```

Leicester m. (2) Rebecca WALDO 12 Feb 1729, Pomfret, CT.
Rebecca, dau. of Daniel WALDO and Susanna ADAMS, b. 5 Feb
1694, Chelmsford, MA; d. 21 May 1753, Pomfret, Windham Co.,
CT.

Children:
```
 +  19 M  vii  Leicester GROSVENOR Jr.
    20 F  viii Rebecca GROSVENOR, b. 30 Nov 1732, Pomfret,
               Windham, CT; d. 21 May 1753.
```

7   Ebenezer GROSVENOR, b. 9 Oct 1684, Roxbury, CT; d. 29 Sep
     1730, Pomfret, CT.
          Ebenezer served as sergeant in a military company at
     Pomfret and was on a committee to build the first schoolhouse
     in Pomfret in 1720. (Bowen)
          Ebenezer GROSVENOR m. Anne MARCY 26 Dec 1707, Woodstock,
     CT. Anne, dau. of John MARCY and Sarah HADLOCK, b. 11 Oct
     1687, Roxbury, MA; d. 30 Jul 1743, Pomfret, Windham Co., CT.

Children:
```
    21 F  i    Susanna GROSVENOR, b. 31 Oct 1708, Pomfret, Windham
               Co., Ma.   She  m.  David  MILLARD  26  Jun  1731,
               Rheobeth, Ma.
 +  22 M  ii   Capt. John GROSVENOR.
 +  23 M  iii  Ebenezer GROSVENOR, Jr.
 +  24 M  iv   Caleb GROSVENOR.
    25 M  v    Joshua GROSVENOR, b. 6 Mar 1718, Pomfret, Windham
               Co., CT; d. 9 May 1724.
```

7

    26 M vi   Moses GROSVENOR, b. 22 Jan 1721, Pomfret, CT., d. 5
               Feb 1725, Pomfret, CT.
    27 F vii   Ann GROSVENOR, b. 14 Sep 1724, Pomfret, Windham
               Co., Ct. She m. Nathaniel DANIEL 20 Oct 1741,
               Pomfret, CT.
    28 M viii Moses GROSVENOR, b. 30 Jun 1729, Pomfret, CT; d. 18
               Feb 1730, Pomfret, CT.

8   Thomas GROSVENOR, b. 30 Sep 1690, Roxbury, MA; d. 30 Sep 1750,
     Pomfret, CT. He m. Elizabeth PEPPER 22 May 1718, Pomfret, Ct.
     Elizabeth, dau. of Jacob PEPPER and Elizabeth PAINE, b. 1694;
     d. 23 Dec 1770.

Children:
    29 F i   Elizabeth GROSVENOR, b. 27 Apr 1720, Pomfret,
               Windham Co., CT; d. 22 Jul 1726.
    30 M ii   William GROSVENOR, b. 25 Aug 1721; d. 23 Jul 1781.
 + 31 M iii   Amos GROSVENOR.
 + 32 M iv   Joshua GROSVENOR.
    33 F v   Elizabeth GROSVENOR, b. 12 Dec 1728, Pomfret,
               Windham Co., CT; d. 7 Sep 1743.
    34 M vi   Robert GROSVENOR

THIRD GENERATION

19   Leicester GROSVENOR Jr., b. 4 Oct 1729, Pomfret, Windham Co.,
     MA., d. 8 Jun 1808, Fairfax, Franklin Co., VT; bur., Safford
     Cem.
          Leicester GROSVENOR Jr. was an ensign in the Connecticut
     militia in 1767. He moved to Windsor, Massachusetts, where he
     served as Captain of militia and as a delegate to the
     convention that adopted the Massachusetts constitution on 12
     Nov 1780. At Windsor he served three short hitches in the
     Revolutionary War - 17 days according to Massachusetts service
     records. He moved to Fairfax, Vermont, where he was recorded
     on the Census of 1791. The records of the town clerk of
     Fairfax show that he purchased 43 acres from Joseph Beaman on
     10 May 1806 for $200, also that he made nine land sales
     between 1795 and 1807. He was paid in pounds and shillings
     for his first five sales and payment for the others was in
     dollars.
          An interesting sale was made on 2 Feb 1795 when he sold
     a piece of land on the Great Brook at Fairfax. The land
     carried a grist mill privilege and the right to build and
     support a dam high enough to accomodate the grist mill but not
     high enough to injure the saw mill of Leicester Grosvenor Jr.
          On 12 Feb 1798 Leicester won a court suit against Asa
     Safford and was awarded three dollars by the Justice of the
     Peace. Asa was also required to pay $1.02 in court costs and
     25 cents and expenses to the Sheriff if it was necessary for
     him to enforce payment. If the Sheriff could find no saleable

property in Asa's possession he was to put Asa in prison at Vergennes in the County of Addison to safely keep him until he paid the necessary sums or was discharged by Leicester Grosvenor Jr. or otherwise by law. (Fairfax Town Records) Leicester GROSVENOR Jr. m. Esther WELD 20 Sep 1753, Pomfret, CT. Esther, dau of John WELD and Esther WALDO, b. 30 Jul 1728, Pomfret, CT; d. 14 Sep 1810, Fairfax, Vt; Bur., Safford Cem.

Children:
+   35 M i   Theophilus GROSVENOR.
+   36 M ii   Resolved GROSVENOR
       37 F III   Esther GROSVENOR, b. 9 Aug 1759, Pomfret, Windham
                   Co., CT. She m. Benjamin CONVERSE 17 May 1786,
                   Hardwicke, MA. Benjamin, son of James CONVERSE and
                   Mary LEAVENS, b. 1746, Thompson, CT; c. 14 Sep
                   1746; d. 1790, Marietta (near), OH.
+   38 M iv   Leicester GROSVENOR, twin.
       39 F v   Rebecca GROSVENOR, twin, b. 11 Aug 1761, Pomfret,
                   CT.   She   m.   John   NEWBERRY   20   May   1790,
                   Williamstown, MA. Four oldest children born at
                   Fairfax, VT. Others born at Stockton, NY. (Bowen)
       40 M vi   Richard GROSVENOR, b. 6 Apr 1765, Pomfret, CT., d.
                   12 Aug 1838, Stockton, NY.
                   Richard is on the federal census of Fairfax,
                   Vermont in 1800, 00011-20011. This is his only
                   record of children.
                   Richard GROSVENOR m. Rebecca GLOYD, Jericho, VT.
                   Rebecca, b. 19 Aug 1764, Abington, CT; d. 13 Jul
                   1827, Stockton, NY.
       41 F vii   Mary GROSVENOR, b. 3 Jun 1768, Pomfret, CT; d. 11
                   Jan 1815, Jericho, VT.
                   She m. Jesse GLOYD 1796. Jesse, b. 17 Apr 1770,
                   Abington, CT; d. 30 Oct 1847.
       42 F viii   Lucy GROSVENOR, b. 15 Nov 1770, Pomfret, CT; d. 25
                   Feb 1844, Stockton, NY.
                   She m. Samuel CRISSEY, Fairfax, VT. Samuel, son of
                   John CRISSEY and Martha DEVENGERT, b. 2 Mar 1770,
                   Stamford, CT., d. 1 Mar 1848, Stockton, NY.
                   Children were: Almira, Harlow, Jason, Lucy,
                   Cynthia, Patty and Samuel.

22   Capt. John GROSVENOR, b. 22 May 1711, Pomfret, CT: d. 3 Feb
       1804, Pomfret, CT.
           John was a Captain of the Pomfret Militia. He served as
       a Captain in the French and Indian War from 1755-1757. He
       served as Selectman four times, Justice of the Peace for 3
       years and a member of the General Assembly in 1755 and 1763.
       He was chairman of a committee to raise clothing for the army
       in 1781. (Bowen) (Burke)

THIRD GENERATION

Capt. John GROSVENOR m. Hannah DRESSER 4 May 1733.
Hannah, dau. of Jonathan DRESSER and Sarah LEAVER, b. 19 Aug
1711, Thompson, CT; d. 1 Aug 1782, Pomfret, CT.

Children:
+   43 M i   John GROSVENOR Jr.
     44 M ii   Nathan GROSVENOR, b. 26 Jun 1735, Pomfret, CT; d.
                20 Jun 1738.
     45 F iii Hannah GROSVENOR, b. 3 Feb 1737, Pomfret, CT; d. 15
                Sep 1790, Woodstock, CT.
                She m. Nathaniel MARCY 11 Sep 1760. Nathaniel, b.
                25 Feb 1733, Woodstock, CT; d. 29 Nov 1790.
     46 M iv   Nathan GROSVENOR, b. 23 Jan 1739 Pomfret, Windham
                Co., CT, d. 3 Jul 1764.
                He married Mary HOLBROOK 10 May 1764. Mary, b.
                1742, d. 30 Oct 1765, bur. E. Woodstock, CT.
     47 F v   Prudence GROSVENOR, b. 16 Dec 1741, Pomfret,
                Windham Co., CT; d. 23 Sep 1743, Pomfret, Windham
                Co., CT.
+   48 M vi   Thomas GROSVENOR.
+   49 M vii Seth GROSVENOR.
     50 M viii Abel GROSVENOR, b. 2 Mar 1749, Pomfret, Windham,
                CT; d. 6 Jan 1780. He died unmarried in the
                Revolutionary War. (Bowen)

23   Ebenezer GROSVENOR Jr., b. 12 Dec 1713, Pomfret, Windham, CT;
     d. 2 Aug 1793.
           He m. Lucy CHENEY 15 Mar 1737. Lucy, dau. of Abiel
     CHENEY and Marian WALDO, b. 20 Oct 1720, Pomfret, Windham, Ct;
     d. 13 May 1791; bur. Hall Cemetery, Pomfret, CT

Children:
+   51 M i   Rev. Ebenezer GROSVENOR.
     52 F ii   Elizabeth GROSVENOR, b. 19 Dec 1740, Pomfret,
                Windham Co., CT; d. 28 Dec 1792, Woodstock, Ct.
                She m. Ichabod MARCY 14 Apr 1763. Ichabod, b. 27
                Dec 1737, Woodstock, CT; d. 12 Sep 1803.
+   53 M iii Oliver GROSVENOR
+   54 M iv   Rev. Asa GROSVENOR.
     55 F v   Lucy GROSVENOR, b. 25 Jul 1747, Pomfret, Windham
                Co., CT; d. 30 Jan 1782, Brookfield, MA. She m.
                Gad WILLISTON May 1771, Pomfret, Windham Co., CT;
                d. 30 Jan 1782, Brookfield, Ma.
                Children were: Joseph, Lucy, Hannah, Joseph
                (again), Joseph (again), and Chloe.
+   56 M vi   Daniel GROSVENOR.
+   57 M vii Lemuel GROSVENOR.
+   58 M viii Ezra GROSVENOR.
     59 F ix   Chloe GROSVENOR, b. 29 Oct 1757, Pomfret, Windham
                Co., CT: d. 4 Apr 1841, Sutton, MA. She m. (____)
                24 Nov 1785.
+   60 M x   Rev. Nathan GROSVENOR

10

24   Caleb GROSVENOR, b. 15 Aug 1716, Pomfret, Windham Co., CT; d.
      20 Apr 1788. In 1753 Caleb had the first choice of pews in
      the new church at Abington as he paid the "largest taxes."
      (Bowen)
           Caleb GROSVENOR m. Sarah CARPENTER 30 Nov 1739. Sarah,
      b. 7 May 1720, Woodstock, CT; d. 11 Feb 1793.

Children:
+   61 M i   Moses GROSVENOR.
     62 F ii   Sarah GROSVENOR, b. 15 Jul 1743, Pomfret, Windham
                 Co., CT; d. 4 May 1829, Brimfield, MA.
                 She m. Alexander SESSIONS Jr. 24 Feb 1774, Pomfret,
                 Windham Co., CT. Alexander, b. 15 Dec 1751,
                 Woodstock, CT; d. 9 Nov 1823, Brimfield, MA.
     63 F iii   Priscilla GROSVENOR, b. 14 Apr 1745, Pomfret,
                 Windham Co., CT; d. 15 Dec 1745.
     64 M iv   Caleb GROSVENOR, b. 15 Oct 1746, Pomfret, Windham
                 Co., CT; d. 31 Mar 1751.
     65 F v   Priscilla (again) GROSVENOR, b. 15 Oct 1748,
                 Pomfret, Windham Co., Ct; d. 7 Oct 1825.
+   66 M vi   Caleb GROSVENOR, Jr.
     67 M vii   Joseph GROSVENOR, b. 18 Feb 1754, Pomfret, Windham
                 Co., CT; d. 25 Oct 1784.
     68 M viii   Darius GROSVENOR, b. 17 Aug 1756.
+   69 M ix   Chester GROSVENOR

31   Amos GROSVENOR, b. 2 Feb 1723, Pomfret, Windham, CT.; d. 3 Jan
      1799, Pomfret, Windham, CT. Amos resided at Spauldings Hill,
      Pomfret. (Bowen)
           Amos GROSVENOR m. Mary HUTCHINS 1 May 1755, Mary, b.
      1727; d. 5 Aug 1770.

Children:
     70 F i   Mary GROSVENOR, b. 10 Feb 1756, Pomfret, Windham,
                 CT; d. 5 Sep 1777.
                 She m. William CHANDLER 6 Feb 1777. William, son
                 of William CHANDLER Jr. and Mary HODGES.
     71 M ii   Amos GROSVENOR, b. 6 Sep 1758, Pomfret, Windham,
                 CT; d. 26 Oct 1776.
     72 F iii   Jerusha GROSVENOR, b. 30 Mar 1761, Pomfret,
                 Windham, CT; d. 18 Sep 1765, Pomfret, Windham Co.,
                 CT.
     73 F iv   Phebe GROSVENOR, b. 22 Nov 1762, Pomfret, Windham,
                 CT; d. 11 Sep 1769
     74 M v   Pearley GROSVENOR, b. 28 Apr 1765, Pomfret,
                 Windham, CT; d. 15 Mar 1787. He graduated from
                 Yale in 1785 and afterwards was a student of
                 theology. (Bowen)
+   75 M vi   Benjamin Hutchens GROSVENOR.
+   76 M vii   Capt. Thomas GROSVENOR.

THIRD GENERATION

32   Joshua GROSVENOR, b. 10 May 1726, Pomfret, Windham Co., CT; d.
      21 Oct 1799.
           Joshua served as first clerk of the Abington School
      Society and clerk of Abington Church and as a member of the
      legislature in 1782. (Bowen)
           Joshua GROSVENOR m. Esther PAYSON 31 Jan 1751. Esther,
      dau. of Edward PAYSON and Thankful HOLMES, b. 29 Sep 1731,
      Pomfret, Windham, CT; d. 17 Jan 1796.

Children:
      77 F i   Elizabeth GROSVENOR, b. 14 Jan 1752.
                  She m. Timeus PIERCE 4 May 1779. Timeus, son of
                  Benjamin PIERCE and Naomi RICHARDS, b. 3 Jun 1751,
                  Canterbury, CT.
      78 F ii   Esther GROSVENOR, b. 6 Jan 1754, Pomfret, Windham
                  Co., CT; d. 3 Apr 1827.
                  She m. Amasa SESSIONS 14 Dec 1775. Amasa, son of
                  Capt. Amasa SESSIONS and Hannah MILLER, b. 12 Aug
                  1748, Pomfret, Windham Co., CT.
      79 M iii   Payson GROSVENOR, b. 25 Feb 1756, Pomfret, Windham
                  Co., CT; d. 5 Oct 1756, Pomfret, Windham Co., CT.
+   80 M iv   Joshua GROSVENOR Jr.
      81 F v   Olive GROSVENOR, b. 17 May 1760, Pomfret, Windham
                  Co., CT; d. 1 Apr 1782.
                  She m. Simeon INGALLS 23 Aug 1781. Simeon, son of
                  Ephraim INGALLS and Mary SHARPE, b. 28 May 1754,
                  Pomfret, Windham Co., CT; d. 26 May 1816.
      82 M vi   Jacob GROSVENOR, b. 20 Jun 1762, Pomfret, Windham
                  Co., CT; d. 9 May 1767, Pomfret, Windham Co., CT.
+   83 M vii   William GROSVENOR, MD.
      84 M viii   Jacob GROSVENOR, b. 4 Jun 1767, Pomfret, Windham
                  Co., CT; d. 8 Sep 1793; bur. Cherry Valley, NY.
      85 M ix   Gratis GROSVENOR, b. 7 Feb 1770, Pomfret, Windham
                  Co., CT; d. 28 Feb 1843.
+   86 M x   Robert GROSVENOR, MD.

FOURTH GENERATION

35   Theophilus GROSVENOR, b. 29 Jul 1755, Pomfret, Windham Co.,
      CT; d. 8 Oct 1797, Fairfax, Franklin Co., VT; bur. Safford
      Cem, Fairfax, VT.
           He enlisted as a drummer boy in the American Revolution
      on 26 April 1778, and served three short enlistments. Upon
      his death his estate passed to Royal, Samuel and Daniel.
      There is no stone marking his grave at Safford Cemetery.
      (Abbey Grosvenor) (Bowen)
           Theophilus GROSVENOR m. Bathsheba THORNTON 28 Oct 1784,
      Windsor, MA. Bathsheba, b. 20 Jul 1765, Lanesboro, MA; d. 8
      Mar 1802, Fairfax, Franklin Co., VT; bur. Safford Cem,
      Fairfax, VT. The Census of 1800 shows that Bathsheba
      Grosvenor was the informant of a household of twenty. The
      census record was 11333-11313-00. This must have been at the

12

large house that my Aunt Clifford photographed in 1936. It
was supposed to be the house where Daniel Grosvenor was born.
Bathsheba and her children account for seven of the residents
and her in-laws account for two more. (RBG)

Children:
    87 M i   Royal GROSVENOR, twin, b. 4 May 1789, Fairfax, Vt.
                Federal Census of 1830 of Miami Co., OH shows Royal
                Grosvenor.
    88 F ii   Abigail GROSVENOR, twin, b. 4 May 1789, Fairfax,
                VT; d. 13 Feb 1836. She m. (____) BISHOP 13 Feb
                1836.
    89 M iii Samuel GROSVENOR, b. 20 Apr 1791, Fairfax, VT.
                Samuel received one third of the estate of his
                father. (Bowen)
    90 F iv   Betsy GROSVENOR, b. 24 Jul 1793, Fairfax, VT; d. 23
                Sep 1829. She m. (____) WEBSTER.
+   91 M v   Daniel GROSVENOR.
    92 M vi   Theophilus GROSVENOR Jr, b. 1 Jul 1797, Fairfax,
                VT; d. abt Jul 1800.

36   Resolved GROSVENOR, b. 24 Aug 1757, Pomfret, Windham Co., CT.
       Resolved enlisted in the service on 13 Oct 1781. His
company marched from Windsor to Saratoga on alarm. He had 16
days service. (Massachusetts Soldiers and Sailors in the War
of the Revolution)
       Resolved GROSVENOR m. (1) Amelia ORDEN. Amelia, d. Oct
1796.

Children:
    93 M i   William GROSVENOR, b. 1792, Fairfax, Vt; d. 4 Nov
                1860, Fairfax, Vt; bur. Sandersons Cem., Fairfax,
                VT. He m. Mary Ann HIGGINS 25 Jun 1844, Fairfax,
                VT.

Resolved m. (2) Elizabeth STEVENSON. Elizabeth, b. Mar 1760;
d. 27 Aug 1841.

Children:
    94 M ii   Thomas GROSVENOR.
    95 F iii Levina GROSVENOR.
    96 F iv   Martha GROSVENOR.
    97 F v   Elizabeth GROSVENOR.

38   Leicester GROSVENOR, twin, b. 11 Aug 1761, Pomfret, CT; d. 26
Apr 1827, Fairfax, Franklin Co., VT; bur. Bowditch Cem,
Franklin Co., VT. He m. Sarah SAFFORD. Sarah, dau. of Ankum
SAFFORD and (____) PLUMB, b. 24 Mar 1766; d. 23 Jul 1824,
Fairfax, Vt; bur. Bowditch Cem.

Children:
```
     98 M i     Elias GROSVENOR, b. 1786; d. 1788, Fairfax, Vt;
                bur. Safford Cem.
+    99 M ii    Samuel GROSVENOR.
```

43   John GROSVENOR Jr., b. 4 Mar 1734, Pomfret, CT; d. Feeding
     Hill, MA. He m. (1) Abigail DAVIS 21 Aug 1755, Pomfret, CT.
     Abigail, dau. of Matthew DAVIS Jr. and Ann DANA, b. 4 Apr
     1733, Pomfret, CT; d. 15 Apr 1763, Pomfret, CT.

Children:
```
    100 M i     Elijah GROSVENOR, b. 8 Feb 1756, Pomfret, CT.
    101 F ii    Prudence GROSVENOR, b. 28 Feb 1758, Pomfret, CT. d.
                2 Sep 1758, Pomfret, CT.
    102 F iii   Prudence GROSVENOR, b. 10 Mar 1760, Pomfret, CT; d.
                24 Mar 1760, Pomfret, CT
```

John GROSVENOR m. (2) Molly LEE 9 Sep 1765.

Children:
```
    103 F iv    Abigail (Anne) GROSVENOR, b. 23 Jun 1766, Pomfret,
                CT; d. 23 Apr 1845, Buffalo, NY.  She m. Capt Ward
                COTTON 31 Jan 1872, Windsor, MA.  Ward, b. 8 Jul
                1762, Pomfret, CT.
    104 M v     Nathan GROSVENOR, b. 1768; d. 1780.
    105 M vi    John GROSVENOR, b. 26 Feb 1770.
+   106 M vii   Israel GROSVENOR
    107 Mviii   Parker GROSVENOR, b. 6 May 1774.
```

48   Thomas GROSVENOR, b. 20 Sep 1744, Pomfret, CT; d. 11 Jul 1825,
     CT.   Thomas Grosvenor graduated from Yale in 1765 and
     practiced law in Pomfret.
          He joined the 1st Co. 3rd Connecticut Regiment commanded
     by Israel Putman and in the battle of Bunker Hill saw nine
     British soldiers fall before his rifle. He was wounded in the
     right hand and bound it with a white cloth while remaining at
     his position. He and his Negro servant are portrayed in John
     Trumbull's Painting of the battle of Bunker Hill.
          Thomas helped with the capture of Fort Ticonderoga on 10
     May 1775 and was promoted to Captain in 1776. He took part in
     the battles of Long Island, Harlem Heights, Trenton, and
     Princeton. He was promoted to Major in 1777 and fought at
     Germantown and Brandywine. He served at Valley Forge in the
     winter of 1777/8.
          Thomas was promoted to Lt. Colonel in 1778 and fought at
     Monmouth and against the Seneca Indians. He was in charge of
     the 1st Connecticut Regiment and Asst. Adjutant General on
     George Washington's Staff. After the war he was judge of the
     Court of Common Pleas of Windham County, Connecticut, for many

years. He served as Judge of the Probate Court and for twenty
years was a member of the Governor's Council. (Bowen)

Thomas GROSVENOR m. Ann MUMFORD 26 Jun 1785, Newport, RI.
Ann, dau. of Capt. Peter MUMFORD, b. 5 Nov 1764; d. 11 Jun
1820.

Children:
+   108 M i   Thomas Mumford GROSVENOR.
     109 M ii   Peter GROSVENOR, b. 1787, Pomfret, Windham Co., CT;
                d. 26 Sep 1791, Pomfret, Windham Co., CT.
+   110 M iii Maj. Peter GROSVENOR.
     111 M iv   John H. GROSVENOR, b. 1796, Pomfret, Windham Co.,
                CT; d. 3 Jan 1848, New York, NY.
     112 F v   Ann GROSVENOR m. Henry KING. Henry, d. 1865.
                Children: John, Ann, Thomas, Henry, Susan, Harriet
                and Edward.
     113 F vi   Hannah GROSVENOR, b. 19 May 1799; d. 5 Aug 1865,
                Pomfret, Windham Co., CT.
                She m. Edward ELDREDGE 6 Mar 1822. Edward, son of
                Capt. James ELDREDGE and Lucy GALLUP, b. 18 Oct
                1794, Brooklyn, CT; d. 8 Sep 1847, Pomfret, Windham
                Co., CT.
                Children: Mary, Frances, Constance, Henry and
                Helen.

49   Seth GROSVENOR, b. 9 Jan 1747, Pomfret, CT; d. 13 Jan 1808.
     Seth was a Corporal in McClellan's Troop of Horse in
1775. He was a Lt. at Bunker Hill. About 1800 he moved to
New Windsor, Vermont and later to Buffalo, New York. (Bowen)
     Seth GROSVENOR m. Abigail KEYES. Abigail, dau. of
Stephen KEYES and Abigail (_____), b. 16 Aug 1751, Pomfret,
Windham Co., CT.

Children:
     114 M i   Roswell GROSVENOR, b. 23 Jul 1769, Pomfret, Windham
                Co., CT; d. 12 May 1771, Pomfret, Windham Co., CT.
     115 F ii   Martha GROSVENOR, b. 23 Oct 1770, Pomfret, Windham
                Co., CT; d. 20 Dec 1857. She m. Joshua ABBE,
                Hudson, NY. Joshua, son of Phineas ABBE and Mary
                BINGHAM, b. 15 Feb 1775, Windham Co., CT.
                Child: Mary
     116 F iii Lucia GROSVENOR, b. 5 Mar 1772, Pomfret, Windham
                Co., CT; d. 1838, Hudson, NY.
                She m. Elisha WILLIAMS 5 Feb 1795. Elisha, son of
                Ebenezer WILLIAMS and Jerusha PORTER, b. 29 Aug
                1773, Pomfret, Windham Co., CT; d. 29 Jun 1833, New
                York, NY.
+   117 M iv   Godfrey Malbone GROSVENOR.
     118 F v   Polly Keyes GROSVENOR, b. 16 Mar 1775, Pomfret,
                Windham Co., CT.

She m. Frederick STANLEY. Frederick, son of Frederick STANLEY Jr. and Mary HOPKINS, b. 15 Apr 1758, Litchfield, CT; d. 19 Apr 1842, Oswego, NY. Child: Mary Eliza.

119 F vi Betsey GROSVENOR, b. 28 Mar 1777, Pomfret, Windham Co., CT.

120 M vii Thomas Peabody GROSVENOR, b. 20 Dec 1778, Pomfret, Windham Co., CT; d. 23 Apr 1817, Waterloo, MD; bur. Hudson, NY.

Thomas graduated from Yale in 1800. He studied law and was admitted to the bar in 1803. He began the practice of law in Hudson, New York. He was in the state legislature 1810-1812 and a Federalist member of Congress 1813-1817. He then engaged in the practice of law at Baltimore until his death at Waterloo. (Who's Who) (Bowen)

Thomas Peabody GROSVENOR m. Mary Jane HANSON Mar 1815. Mary, dau. of Alexander HANSON and Rebecca HOWARD, bur. Hudson, NY.

+ 121 M viii Abel Moore GROSVENOR.

122 F ix Peggy GROSVENOR, b. 9 Mar 1782, Pomfret, Windham Co., Ct; d. 4 May 1782, Pomfret, Windham Co., CT.

123 M x Capt Gordon Henry GROSVENOR, b. 29 Jul 1783, Pomfret, Windham Co., CT. Captain in War of 1812. Served 21 Apr 1814 to 1 Jun 1821. (Bowen)

124 M xi Seth GROSVENOR, b. 25 Dec 1786, Pomfret, Windham Co., CT; d. 4 Oct 1857.

Seth was a merchant at Buffalo, NY and in New York City. At Buffalo he was in partnership with his brothers Abel and Stephen and his brother-in-law Rueben Heacock. Seth moved to New York in 1816 and was a dry goods merchant and a director of the Farmers Loan and Trust Co.

At Buffalo Seth founded the Grosvenor Library which after 1935 became part of the Erie County Library. The Library owns a portrait of Seth painted by Thomas LeClear. Later portraits are owned by the Buffalo Historical Society and by the Misses Grosvenor. (Bowen)

125 F xii Abigail Peabody GROSVENOR, b. 3 Jun 1788, Pomfret, Windham Co., CT; d. 4 Dec 1868. She m. Reuben B. HEACOCK. Reuben, son of Reuben HEACOCK and Silence EASTON, b. 1789, Durham, CT; d. 4 Apr 1854. Children: Abby, Seth, Abel, Mary, Thomas, Reuben, Grosvenor Williams, Stephen, and Abby Eliza.

126 M xiii Stephen Keyes GROSVENOR, b. 10 Aug 1789, Pomfret, Windham Co., CT; d. 2 May 1790.

127 M xiv Col. Stephen Keyes GROSVENOR, b. 5 Apr 1791, Pomfret, Windham Co., CT; d. 1 Nov 1839, Buffalo, Erie Co., NY. He was Colonel of the 17th Cavalry Regt. organized in Genese Co., NY in 1822. (Bowen)

51   Rev. Ebenezer GROSVENOR, b. 6 Mar 1738; d. 28 May 1788.
        Ebenezer graduated from Yale in 1759 and was a
Congregational minister at Scituate and Harvard, MA. He
received his MA degree from Harvard in 1763. (Bowen)
(Jeanette Grosvenor)
        Rev. Ebenezer GROSVENOR m. Elizabeth CLARK 2 Feb 1764,
Danvers, MA. Elizabeth, dau. of Rev. Peter CLARK and Deborah
HOBART.

Children:
      128 F i   Deborah GROSVENOR, b. 10 Jan 1765, Scituate, MA; d.
               1 Sep 1765.
      129 F ii   Lucy GROSVENOR, b. 4 Jun 1766, Scituate, MA; d. 8
               Feb 1795, Harvard, MA.
      130 M iii Ebenezer GROSVENOR, b. 11 Mar 1768, Scituate, MA;
               d. 15 May 1788, Harvard, MA.
      131 F iv   Elizabeth GROSVENOR, b. 3 Dec 1769, Scituate, MA;
               d. 6 Mar 1773, Scituate, MA.
+   132 M v   Peter Clark GROSVENOR, MD.
      133 F vi   Nancy GROSVENOR, b. 17 Feb 1773, Scituate, MA: d.
               22 Sep 1788, Harvard, MA.
      134 F vii Elizabeth GROSVENOR, b. 18 Jun 1775, Scituate, MA.
      135F viii Mary GROSVENOR, b. 3 Apr 1777. She m. Henry PARKER
               13 Apr 1796.

53   Oliver GROSVENOR, b. 19 May 1743, Pomfret, CT: d. 15 May 1824,
Pomfret, CT. Oliver served as Commissary of Col. Ebenezer
Williams 11th Regt. in the Revolutionary War. (Bowen)
        Oliver GROSVENOR m. Terviah PAYSON 4 May 1771, Pomfret,
CT. Terviah, dau of John PAYSON, d. 15 May 1824.

Children:
      136 M i   Charles GROSVENOR, b. 23 May 1773, Pomfret, Windham
               Co., CT; d. 23 Sep 1773, Pomfret, Windham Co., CT.
+   137 M ii   Charles GROSVENOR.
+   138 M iii Payson GROSVENOR.
      139 F iv   Zerviah GROSVENOR, b. 16 Jun 1779, Pomfret, Windham
               Co., CT; d. 7 Apr 1842. She m. Stephen HUBBARD 19
               Sep 1803. Stephen, son of Maj. Benjamin HUBBARD
               and Chloe ELDRIDGE, b. 19 Sep 1776, Smithfield, RI;
               d. 20 Jun 1853.
               Children: William, Julia, Oliver, Benjamin, and
               Stephen.
+   140 M v   Oliver Clarke GROSVENOR.

54   Rev. Asa GROSVENOR, b. 6 Apr 1745, Pomfret, Windham Co., CT;
d. 28 Dec 1834, Reading, MA. Asa was a Captain in the
Revolutionary War. He lived at Pomfret until 1810 and moved
to Reading. (Jeanette Grosvenor)
        Rev. Asa GROSVENOR m. Hannah HALL 24 Apr 1766, Sutton,
MA.

FOURTH GENERATION

Children:
+ 141 M i Aaron GROSVENOR, MD.
  142 F ii Hannah GROSVENOR, b. 31 Aug 1769, Pomfret, Windham Co., Ct; d. 14 Nov 1843. She m. Dea Joel GODDARD. Joel, son of Robert GODDARD and Elizabeth (____), b. 8 Apr 1763, Petersham, MA; d. 6 Dec. 1843.
  143 M iii Asa GROSVENOR, b. 6 Jan 1772, Pomfret, Windham Co., CT; d. 9 Jan 1772, Pomfret, Windham Co., CT.
  144 F iv Lucy GROSVENOR, b. 28 Jun 1773, Pomfret, Windham Co., CT. She m. Capt Benjamin CARGILL.
  145 M v Asa GROSVENOR, b. 12 Mar 1776.
  146 M vi Rev. Ebenezer Hall GROSVENOR, b. 28 Apr 1778, Pomfret, Windham Co., CT. Rev. Ebenezer was a Methodist Minister and joined the Shakers at New Lebanon, NY.
  147 F vii Betsey GROSVENOR, b. 29 May 1780, Pomfret, Windham Co., CT; d. 9 Jan 1836.
+ 148 M viii David Augustus GROSVENOR, MD.

56 Daniel GROSVENOR, b. 9 Apr 1750, Pomfret, Windham Co., CT; d. 22 Jul 1834, Petersham, MA. Daniel graduated from Yale in 1769 and was a pastor at Grafton. He was also a trustee at Leicester Academy. He served in the Revolutionary War. (Jeanette Grosvenor) (Bowen)
    Daniel GROSVENOR m. (____) 9 May 1776, Sutton, MA

Children:
+ 149 M i Daniel Buckley GROSVENOR.
+ 150 M ii Col David Hall GROSVENOR.
+ 151 M iii Jonathan Prescott GROSVENOR.
  152 F iv Deborah GROSVENOR, b. 9 Dec 1781, Grafton, MA. She m. Larkin NEWTON 1800. Larkin, son of Silas NEWTON and Delia HOWE, b. 1777, Paxton, MA; d. 13 Dec 1805, Paxton, MA.
+ 153 M v Ebenezer Oliver GROSVENOR.
  154 F vi Lucy Williston GROSVENOR, b. 8 Dec 1785, Grafton, MA.
    She m. Rev. Joel WRIGHT 30 Dec 1812. Joel, son of Benjamin WRIGHT and Betsey ADAMS, b. 26 Dec 1784, Milford, NH; d. 8 Jun 1859, S. Hadley Falls, MA. Child: Rev. Daniel Grosvenor WRIGHT.
  155 M vii Ira Rufus GROSVENOR, b. 10 Sep 1787, Grafton, MA; d. 2 Jan 1796.
  156 F viii Elizabeth Sophia GROSVENOR, b. 25 Nov 1789. She m. Ashbel GODDARD 9 May 1816. Ashbel, son of Joel GODDARD and Anna SUTTON, b. 1 Oct 1788, Petersham, MA.
+ 157 M ix Rev. Cyrus Pitt GROSVENOR.
  158 M x Rev. Moses Gill GROSVENOR, b. 23 Sep 1796, Paxton, MA; d. 24 Jul 1879, Worcester, MA. Moses graduated from Dartmouth in 1822, and from Andover in 1825. He served at churches in Massachusetts, New Hampshire, Vermont, and New York. (Bowen)

18

Rev. Moses Gill GROSVENOR m. Sophia W. GROUT 10 Feb 1830.

57   Lemuel GROSVENOR, b. 11 Aug 1752, Pomfret, Windham Co., CT; d. 19 Jan 1833, Pomfret, Windham Co., CT.
      Lemuel served in the Revolutionary War and fought at Bunker Hill under General Putman. He was promoted to Lt. in 1778 and to Purchaser in 1780. Later he served as Judge of Probate and was commissioned Brig. General of Militia. He was appointed Postmaster of Pomfret by President Washington on 1 Jan 1795 and served in that position for nearly forty years until his death. He was a member of the legislature in 1794 and 1796. He helped to form the Atwater-Lyon Company at New Haven to manufacture 'woollen' cloth. The company was to be tax exempt for five years. At his death he bequeathed to the Connecticut Historical Society the sword used by General Putman. (Bowen)
      Lemuel GROSVENOR m. (1) Eunice (Putman) AVERY 7 Sep 1783, Brooklyn, CT. Eunice, b. 19 Jun 1740; d. 27 Jun 1799.

Children:
+   159 M i   Lemuel Putman Grosvenor.
     160 M ii   Guy GROSVENOR, b. 5 Sep 1786, Pomfret, Windham Co., CT; d. 10 Sep 1788.
     161 M iii Ebenezer GROSVENOR, b. 26 Jul 1788, Pomfret, Windham Co., CT; d. 10 Nov 1817. Ebenezer was a lawyer in Pomfret. (Bowen)
                Ebenezer GROSVENOR m. Harriet PUTMAN 3 May 1815.
     162 M iv   Clark Guy GROSVENOR, b. 23 May 1790, Pomfret, Windham Co., CT; d. 16 Oct 1809.
     163 M v   Lewis GROSVENOR, b. 12 Apr 1794, Pomfret, Windham Co., CT; d. 12 Aug 1833.

Lemuel m. (2) Sarah PERKINS 9 Mar 1801. Sarah, dau. of Elisha PERKINS and Sarah DOUGLAS, b. 26 Oct 1771, Norwich, CT; d. 16 Oct 1831.

Children:
     164 M vi   Perkins GROSVENOR, b. 25 Apr 1802, Pomfret, Windham, CT; d. 28 Apr 1802, Pomfret, Windham, CT.
     165 F vii Eunice GROSVENOR, b. 23 Aug 1803, Pomfret, Windham, CT; d. 5 Jul 1883.
     166 F viii Sarah Perkins GROSVENOR, b. 5 Feb 1806, Pomfret, Windham, CT; d. 31 Jan 1891.
                She m. Col Charles COIT 14 Oct 1834. Charles, son of Nathaniel COIT and Betsey MORGAN, b. 19 Feb 1793, Preston, CT; d. 26 Oct 1855.
                Children: Ellen, Charles, Sarah Perkins and George Douglas.
     167 F ix   Ellen Douglas GROSVENOR, b. 27 Feb 1814, Pomfret, Windham, CT; d. 10 Nov 1831.

58   Ezra GROSVENOR, b. 23 Jun 1755, Pomfret, Windham Co., CT; d.
      8 Jul 1827, Pittsburg, PA.
            Ezra served in the Revolutionary War. He lived at
      Pomfret, and Mansfield, Connecticut and Bridgewater, Vermont.
      He manufactured sewing silk at Mansfield. (Bowen)
            Ezra GROSVENOR m. Sarah CARPENTER 4 May 1786, Ashford,
      CT. Sarah, dau. of John CARPENTER and Mary LOOMIS, b. 4 Apr
      1760, Stafford, CT; d. 18 Nov 1813, Bridgewater, VT.

Children:
      168 M i   Ezra GROSVENOR, Jr., b. 7 Apr 1787, Pomfret,
                  Windham Co., CT.
      169 M ii   Roswell GROSVENOR, b. 26 Jan 1788, Pomfret, Windham
                  Co., CT
      170 M iii   Rufus GROSVENOR.
      171 M iv   Chauncey GROSVENOR, b. 4 Apr 1792, Pomfret, Windham
                  Co., CT.
      172 M v   Orrin GROSVENOR, b. 20 Mar 1794, Pomfret, Windham
                  Co., CT; d. 29 Jun 1811, Bridgewater, VT.
      173 F vi   Sally GROSVENOR, b. 17 Feb 1796, Pomfret, Windham
                  Co., CT; d. 12 Apr 1886, Chardon, OH.
                  She m. (1) Elisha SANDERSON Feb 1816, Bridgewater,
                  MA. Elisha, son of Phineas SANDERSON and Lucy
                  BURKE, b. 17 Jun 1790; d. 7 Jun 1856.
                  Children: Sarah, Laura, Charles and Emory.
                  Sally GROSVENOR m. (2) Rev. Ira EDDY 18 Mar 1863,
                  Garretsville, OH. Ira, son of Nathan EDDY and
                  Rebecca SAFFORD.
      174 F vii   Lucy GROSVENOR, b. 3 Nov 1798, Pomfret, Windham
                  Co., CT.
      175 F viii Mary GROSVENOR, b. 16 Sep 1800, Pomfret, Windham
                  Co., CT.
      176 F ix   Almira GROSVENOR, b. 31 Aug 1802, Pomfret, Windham
                  Co., CT.
      177 F x   Laura GROSVENOR, b. 19 May 1805, Pomfret, Windham
                  Co., CT.

60   Rev. Nathan GROSVENOR, b. 17 Dec 1764, Pomfret, CT; d. 14 Feb
      1814, Pomfret, CT. Rev. Nathan was a deacon at Craftsbury,
      Vermont and later became a Congregational minister. (Jeanette
      Grosvenor)
            Rev. Nathan GROSVENOR m. Lydia ADAMS 13 Nov 1788. Lydia,
      b. 16 Oct 1768; d. 1857.

Children:
      178 F i   Laura GROSVENOR, b. 30 Oct 1789, Pomfret, Windham
                  Co., CT. She m. William CLARK 8 Apr 1813, Hampton,
                  CT.
      179 F ii   Lydia GROSVENOR, b. 5 Aug 1791, Pomfret, Windham
                  Co., CT; d. 6 Jul 1873, Freedom, Portage Co., OH;
                  bur. Drakesburg, OH.
+   180 M iii   Nathan Ebenezer GROSVENOR.
      181 M iv   Mason GROSVENOR, b. 15 Apr 1796, Pomfret, Windham
                  Co., CT; d. 30 Oct 1796, Pomfret, Windham Co., CT.

```
      182 F  v   Lucy GROSVENOR, b. 8 Nov 1797, Pomfret, Windham
                    Co., CT.
  +   183 M  vi  Rev. Mason GROSVENOR.
  +   184 M  vii Rev. David Adams GROSVENOR.
      185F viii Mary Eliza GROSVENOR, b. abt 1809, Craftsbury, VT;
                    d. 14 Feb 1814, Chaplin, CT.
```

61   Moses GROSVENOR, b. 11 Aug 1741; d. 16 Mar 1811, Grosvenors
     Cor., Carlisle, NY.
          Moses joined the army on 16 June 1782. He had six days
     sevice against insurgents at Springfield and Northhampton.
     (Mass. Soldiers and Sailors in the War of the Revolution)
          Moses GROSVENOR m. Dorcas SHARPE 10 Jan 1765, Abington,
     CT. Dorcas, dau. of John SHARPE and Dorcas DAVIS, b. 20 Jan
     1738; d. 11 Apr 1821, Brimfield, MA.

Children:
```
  +   186 M  i   Willard GROSVENOR
      187 F  ii  Clarissa GROSVENOR, b. 4 Dec 1767, Pomfret, Windham
                    Co., CT.  She m. Isaiah COOK 6 Jun 1796,
                    Lawyersville, NY.  Isaiah, son of Joshua COOK and
                    Mary (____), b. 18 Jul 1768, Chatham, CT.
      188 M  iii Percy GROSVENOR, b. 1 Sep 1771, Pomfret, Windham
                    Co., CT; d. 11 Jan 1773, Pomfret, Windham Co., CT.
  +   189 M  iv  Moses GROSVENOR Jr.
  +   190 M  v   Amasa GROSVENOR.
      191 M  vi  Charles GROSVENOR, b. 14 May 1779, Pomfret, Windham
                    Co., CT; d. 26 Feb 1863.  He m. Lucy BROWN 6 Jun
                    1805, Ryders Cor., NY.  Lucy, b. 3 Jan 1785; d. 23
                    Jan 1869.
```

66   Caleb GROSVENOR Jr., b. 4 Aug 1751, Pomfret, Windham Co., CT;
          d. 3 Sep 1807, Lanesboro, MA. Caleb responded as a
          private to the Lexington alarm of April 1775 and served
          eleven days during the Revolutionary War. (Bowen)
          Caleb GROSVENOR Jr. m. Olive GRIFFIN 11 Jan 1776,
     Pomfret, Windham Co., CT. Olive, b. 1751; d. 1828.

Children:
```
      192 F  i   Persis GROSVENOR, b. 22 Nov 1776, Pomfret, Windham
                    Co., CT.  She m. William WOLCOTT 12 Feb 1802,
                    Lanesboro, MA.
      193 F  ii  Olive GROSVENOR, b. 2 Nov 1778, Pomfret, Windham
                    Co., CT.
  +   194 M  iii Ebenezer Griffin GROSVENOR.
  +   195 M  iv  Vine GROSVENOR
```

69   Chester GROSVENOR, b. 28 Jul 1758, Pomfret, Windham Co., CT.
     He m. Mary LYON 11 Jan 1776. Mary, b. 23 Jan 1760, Pomfret,
     Windham Co., CT.

Children:
```
      196 M  i   Joseph GROSVENOR, b. 18 Apr 1785, Pomfret, Windham
                    Co., CT.
```

197 M ii   Silas GROSVENOR, b. 4 Mar 1787, Pomfret, Windham
           Co., CT.
198 F iii Mary GROSVENOR.

75   Benjamin Hutchins GROSVENOR, b. 4 Aug 1770; d. 23 Apr 1847.
      He m. Chloe TROWBRIDGE 24 Feb 1795. Chloe, dau. of John
TROWBRIDGE and Anna KINNEY, b. 29 Mar 1772, Abington; d. 26
Oct 1826.

Children:
    199 M i   John Trowbridge GROSVENOR, b. 18 Jan 1796, Pomfret,
             Windham Co., CT; d. 15 Jan 1797, Pomfret, Windham
             Co., CT.
    200 F ii   Mary Anna GROSVENOR, b. 21 Oct 1797, Pomfret,
             Windham Co., CT; d. 22 May 1818.
    201 F iii   Hannah GROSVENOR, b. 21 Dec 1799, Pomfret, Windham
             Co., CT; d. 17 Sep 1828.
    202 F iv   Jerusha GROSVENOR, b. Jul 1802, Pomfret, Windham
             Co., CT; d. 10 Mar 1824.
    203 M v   Benjamin Hutchins GROSVENOR, b. 18 Sep 1804,
             Pomfret, Windham Co., CT; d. 27 Jul 1834.
+   204 M vi   John Williams GROSVENOR.
    205 F vii   Emily Adaline GROSVENOR, b. 5 May 1809, Pomfret,
             Windham Co., CT; d. 21 Feb 1898. She m. Col.
             Horace SABIN 24 Mar 1836. Horace, son of Horatio
             SABIN and Elizabeth WILLIAMS, b. 11 Mar 1810,
             Pomfret, Windham Co., CT; d. 30 Oct 1894.
  206 F viii Althea Marie GROSVENOR, b. 15 Nov 1812, Pomfret,
             Windham Co., CT; d. 8 May 1892.

76   Capt. Thomas GROSVENOR, b. 1 Mar 1757, Pomfret, Windham Co.,
CT; d. 15 Dec 1843.
      Captain Thomas GROSVENOR served in the Revolutionary War
and lived at Abington. He served in the Legislature in 1792,
1793, 1799, 1801 and 1804. (Bowen)
      Capt. Thomas GROSVENOR m. (1) Althea GROSVENOR 3 Jun
1784. Althea, b. 11 May 1762, Pomfret, Windham Co., CT; d. 8
May 1789.

Children:
    207 M i   Pearley GROSVENOR, b. 13 Jan 1788, Pomfret, Windham
             Co., CT; d. 18 Aug 1791, Pomfret, Windham Co., CT.

Capt. Thomas GROSVENOR m. (2) Theoda PERRIN 11 Dec 1800.
Theoda, dau of Capt David PERRIN and Esther MARCY, b. 4 Mar
1773, Woodstock, CT.

Children:
    208 M ii   Thomas GROSVENOR, b. 21 Sep 1802, Pomfret, Windham
             Co., CT; d. 24 Dec 1806, Pomfret, Windham Co., CT.
    209 F iii   Pearley GROSVENOR, b. 4 Sep 1805, Pomfret, Windham
             Co., CT.
+   210 M iv   Capt Thomas GROSVENOR.

211 F v   Mary Hutchins GROSVENOR, b. 15 Apr 1812, Pomfret,
          Windham Co., CT; d. 12 Jun 1814.

80   Joshua GROSVENOR Jr., b. 25 Apr 1758; d. 2 Apr 1838.   He m.
     Sarah INGALLS 10 Feb 1784.   Sarah, dau. of Ephraim INGALLS and
     Mary SHARPE, b. 17 Feb 1762, Pomfret, Windham Co., CT; d. 10
     May 1807.

Children:
     212 F i   Olive GROSVENOR, b. 14 Nov 1784, Pomfret, Windham
                Co., CT; d. 17 Nov 1872.   She m. John OSGOOD 17 Mar
                1808.   John, son of Capt William OSGOOD and Mary
                SCARBOROUGH, b. 13 Mar 1782, Abington, MA; d. 19
                Dec 1872, Cincinnatus, NY.
     213 M ii   Payson GROSVENOR, b. 1 Jul 1786, Pomfret, Windham
                Co., CT; d. 17 Nov 1872, Pomfret, Windham Co., CT.
     214 F iii Sally GROSVENOR, b. 28 May 1788, Pomfret, Windham
                Co., CT; d. 29 Apr 1837.   She m. Joshua REYNOLDS.
+   215 M iv   Payson Jasper GROSVENOR.
     216 M v   Walter GROSVENOR, b. 13 Sep 1792, Pomfret, Windham
                Co., CT; d. 11 Oct 1796.
+   217 M vi   Jasper GROSVENOR.
     218 F vii Esther GROSVENOR, b. 11 Nov 1796, Pomfret, Windham
                Co., CT; d. 12 Sep 1820.
     219F viii Deborah GROSVENOR, b. 15 Dec 1798, Pomfret, Windham
                Co., CT; d. 1 Feb 1799.
+   220 M ix   Charles Ingalls GROSVENOR.
     221 M x   Joshua GROSVENOR, b. 10 Apr 1804, Pomfret, Windham
                Co., CT; d. 14 Apr 1804.

83   William GROSVENOR, MD, b. 21 Aug 1764, Pomfret, Windham Co.,
     CT; d. 16 Oct 1798, Tolland, MA.
          He m. Mary WILLIAMS 4 Oct 1787.   Mary, dau. of Rev.
     Nathan WILLIAMS and Mary HALL, b. 19 Apr 1768, Tolland, MA.

Children:
     222 F i   Mary Williams GROSVENOR, b. Tolland, MA.
     223 F ii   Ruth GROSVENOR, b. Tolland, MA.
     224 M iii Jacob GROSVENOR.

86   Robert GROSVENOR, MD, b. 27 Aug 1772, Pomfret, Windham Co.,
     CT; d. 20 Oct 1849; bur. N. Killingly, CT.
          Robert GROSVENOR had a house and office building at
     Killingly and was a member of the Windham Co. Medical Society
     and the Connecticut Historical Society.   (Bowen)
          Robert GROSVENOR, MD m. (1) Mary BEGGS.

Children:
+   225 M i   William GROSVENOR, MD.
     226 F ii   Amelia GROSVENOR, b. 1 May 1810, Killingly, d. 11
                May 1810.
     227 F iii Harriet GROSVENOR, b. 1813, Killingly.   She m.
                Jesse Sanford ELY 4 May 1835, Killingly.   Jesse,

Son of Eli ELY and Sarah SANFORD, b. 1807; d. 1879.
Children: William, Edward, and Charles.

Robert GROSVENOR, MD m. (2) Abelena HOWE 25 Jun 1795,
Killingly. Abelena, dau of Samson HOWE and Huldah DAVIS, b.
25 Mar 1775; d. 10 Aug 1796.

Children:
+   228 M iv   Robert Howe GROSVENOR.
     229 F v   Abelena Howe GROSVENOR, b. 1800; d. 3 Dec 1865.
                 She m. Isaac Tompkins HUTCHINS 20 Apr 1826. Isaac,
                 son of Penuel HUTCHINS and Mary THOMPSON, b. 15 Feb
                 1796, Killingly, CT; d. 25 Oct 1884.
                 Children born at West Killingly: Elisha, Mary,
                 Rebecca, Isaac and Robert.
     230 F vi   Mary GROSVENOR, b. 1802 Killingly; d. 29 Oct 1820.
     231 F vii Elizabeth Howe GROSVENOR, b. 1808, Killingly; d. 20
                 Oct 1820.

91   Daniel GROSVENOR, b. 8 May 1795, Fairfax, Franklin Co., VT; d.
     13 Aug 1867, Troy, Miami Co., OH; bur. Rose Hill Cem. Troy,
     OH.
         Daniel was a member of the militia company that was
     organized to protect Fairfax during the War of 1812. On 6 Sep
     1814 the British army, advancing from Canada, was heard
     cannonading Plattsburg. Daniel took his gun and necessary
     provisions and marched with his company to an encampment near
     Plattsburg. They were issued tents and rations and chose
     officers. They joined other companies on a bluff above Lake
     Champlain where they watched a one hour duel between the
     British and American fleets and saw the British flag come
     down.
         They then marched into the woods and up the Saranac River
     and joined other troops in a short fierce encounter with the
     British in which they took 20 prisoners. They slept in the
     woods that night and the next morning crossed the river into
     Plattsburg to pursue the enemy. However it began raining hard
     and the pursuit was abandoned. On Sep 18 his company started
     for home. Later Daniel wrote about his experience in an
     Application for Bounty.
         In June 1818 Daniel joined the Masonic Lodge of Fairfax.
     This was the beginning of a lifetime association with the
     Masons. In 1819 he emigrated to Troy, Miami Co. Ohio. He
     taught school and pursued his legal studies until April 1822
     when he was admitted to the Miami County Bar. He served as
     County Auditor from 1822 to 1829. He received bounty land in
     the Western Reserve of northern Ohio while he was living in
     Troy. He visited the property and decided to stay in Troy.
         Daniel was active in local politics. In 1828 he served
     on a committee for the reelection of John Quincy Adams. In
     1830 he served on the Troy Board of Trustees. One of the
     Trutees' first acts was to proclaim that the owner of a hog
     that was running in the streets was to be fined 25 cents.

After his work as County Auditor he followed the legal profession and operated a store. In 1835 the Troy Lyceum was founded and Daniel took part in debates in the basement of the Episcopal Church. The debaters were mostly doctors, lawyers, and preachers.

In 1843 the Methodists of Troy split over the issue of slavery. The abolitionists of the congregation, including Daniel, broke away and founded the Wesleyan Methodist Church. Daniel made speeches against slavery and the use of alcohol. He also helped fugitive slaves that passed through Troy hidden in the cargo holds of canal boats that traveled the canal from the Ohio River to Lake Erie.

During the Civil War Daniel moved his drug store to Union City, Indiana, under the management of his son Julius. Julius died in 1864 and Daniel sold the store at a loss. Daniel saw his sons Augustus and Chauncey go to war and return.

At the time of Lincoln's death Daniel served on a committee to draw up a resolution of mourning. Flags were to be displayed at half staff for 30 days. On 29 Apr 1865 Lincoln's funeral train passed through Miami County on the way to Springfield, Illinois, for burial. A large crowd of people watched in silence.

Daniel died in Troy in August 1867. His funeral was conducted by the Masons and the Miami Bar Association attended as a body wearing badges of mourning. (Beers) (Grosvenor Documents)

Daniel GROSVENOR m. Frances BARBER 1 Dec 1825, Troy, OH. Frances, b. 29 Jul 1804, Colerain, MA; d. 16 Jul 1884, Troy, Miami Co, OH; bur. Rose Hill Cem. Troy, OH.

Children:
+   232 M i   Julius Thornton GROSVENOR.
     233 F ii   Helen Elizabeth GROSVENOR, b. 3 Sep 1828, Troy, OH;
                 d. 7 Jul 1901, Clorinda, IA; bur., Clorinda, IA.
     234 F iii Juliet Riley GROSVENOR, b. 29 May 1831, Troy, OH;
                 d. 5 Dec 1844, Troy, OH; bur. Rose Hill Cem. Troy,
                 OH.
+   235 F iv   Mary Frances GROSVENOR.
+   236 M v   Augustus Daniel GROSVENOR.
     237 F vi   Electa Lavinie GROSVENOR, b. 27 Aug 1840, Troy, OH;
                 d. 19 May 1875 Troy, OH; bur. Rose Hill Cem. Troy,
                 OH.
                 Vinnie was Chauncey's correspondent during the war.
                 She sent him the family news and ten dollars
                 whenever he needed it. She is listed as a Court
                 House Clerk on the Census of 1870. (Chauncey)
+   238 M vii Chauncey Frederick GROSVENOR.

99   Samuel Grosvenor. He m. (_____).

Child:
+   239 M i   Reuben Safford GROSVENOR

106   Israel GROSVENOR, b. 23 May 1772, Pomfret, CT; d. May 1842, Warren Co., PA.

Israel was a cattle buyer and resided in Warren County, Pennsylvania, for 20 years. On 29 March 1842 the "Peoples Monitor" and "Warren Democrat" of Warren, PA carried a full column obituary on Israel. It described him as a man of fine personal appearance and of abilities superior to most men but also as a man who had close association with persons of the worst character and who had gotten the property of other people. (Suzanne Soltess)

Israel GROSVENOR m. Eunice JONES 1793, Poultney, VT. Eunice, dau. of Nathan JONES and Elizabeth BIDWELL, b. bef 3 May 1772, Abington, CT; d. 1866.

Children:
      240 M i   Israel GROSVENOR, b. bef 1795, Poultney, VT.
+   241 M ii   Nathan GROSVENOR.
      242 F iii Marcia P. GROSVENOR, b. 24 Feb 1798, Poultney, VT; d. 19 Feb 1890, Lottsville, Warren Co., PA.
                 She m. (1) Timothy WOODIN abt 1813, Philadelphia, PA. Timothy, son of Amos WOODIN and Mary WILSEY, b. 6 Sep 1793, Monroe Co., NY; d. 1835, Warren Co., PA.
                 Children: Bushrod Washington, Emmett, Eunice, Timothy, Lucia, Julia, Russell, Mary.
                 Marcia P. GROSVENOR m. (2) John BAILEY.
                 Children: Charles and Nathan.
      243 F iv   Lucia GROSVENOR, b. aft 1798.
      244 M v   Russel GROSVENOR, b. aft 1799.
      245 M vi   John GROSVENOR, b. aft 1800.
                 John assisted in stealing $4000 in bank notes and was tried and convicted even though his mother and others in his family swore falsely in order to protect him. He was in prison at the time of his father's death. (Suzanne Soltess)

108 Thomas Mumford GROSVENOR, b. 26 Mar 1786; d. 9 Apr 1867.

Thomas was a member of the Connecticut Legislature in 1829. In 1838 he and his brother Peter moved to Plymouth, Astabula, Ohio where they had adjoining farms. Thomas' five sons served in the Civil War. (Bowen)

Thomas Mumford GROSVENOR m. Charlotte LEE 21 Dec 1824. Charlotte, b. 3 Aug 1799; d. 26 Oct 1888.

Children:
+   246 M i   Thomas GROSVENOR.
+   247 M ii   Capt. Samuel Lee GROSVENOR.
      248 M iii John GROSVENOR, b. 9 Oct 1829, Pomfret, Windham Co., CT; d. 23 Aug 1832, Pomfret, Windham Co., CT.
      249 M iv   Ebenezer GROSVENOR, b. 22 Nov 1831, Pomfret, Windham Co., CT; d. 5 Mar 1834, Pomfret, Windham Co., CT.

250 M v   Capt. Ebenezer GROSVENOR, b. 16 Mar 1834, Pomfret, Windham Co., CT; d. 16 Dec 1864.
He served in 22nd and 18th Ohio Volunteer Infantry (OVI) in the Civil War. He was killed at battle of Nashville while leading the 28th OVI as Acting Colonel. (Bowen)

251 M vi   Frank GROSVENOR, b. 19 Mar 1836, Pomfret, Windham Co., CT. Frank served in 3rd W. Va. Cavalry in Civil War. (Bowen)

252 M vii   David GROSVENOR, b. 15 Sep 1838; d. 29 Dec 1863.
Captain David was a private and a Captain in the 36th Ohio regiment. He fought at Bull Run, South Mountain, Antietam, Hoover's Gap, Chickamauga, Brown's Ferry and Missionary Ridge. He was wounded in the last battle and died in the tent of his cousin Gen. Charles H. GROSVENOR one month after the battle. (Bowen)

110   Maj Peter GROSVENOR, b. 25 Jan 1794, Pomfret, Windham Co., CT; d. Sep 1859.
      Peter was a Major in the 10th Connecticut Regiment in the War of 1812. He moved with his family to Athens, Ohio in 1838. (Bowen)
      Maj. Peter GROSVENOR m. Ann CHASE 26 Jan 1820. Ann, dau. of Abner CHASE and Sarah LEVIN, b. 26 Apr 1794, Swansea, MA; d. 8 Apr 1881.

Children:

253 F i   Ann Mumford GROSVENOR, b. 1 Oct 1820, Pomfret, Windham Co., CT; d. 29 Jan 1823, Pomfret, Windham Co., Ct.

254 M ii   Thomas GROSVENOR, b. 31 Aug 1822, Pomfret, Windham Co., CT; d. 17 Sep 1824, Pomfret, Windham Co., CT.

255 F iii   Ann Mumford (again) GROSVENOR, b. 22 Aug 1824, Pomfret, Windham Co., CT; d. 29 May 1826, Pomfret, Windham Co., CT.

256 F iv   Anna Maria GROSVENOR, b. 19 Sep 1826, Pomfret, Windham Co., CT; d. 2 Dec 1831, Pomfret, Windham Co., CT.

257 F v   Julia Elizabeth GROSVENOR, b. 19 Feb 1829, Pomfret, Windham Co., CT; d. 22 Nov 1831, Pomfret, Windham Co., CT.

258 M vi   John Mumford GROSVENOR, b. 22 Oct 1832, Pomfret, Windham Co., CT.
John was a private, 1st and 2nd Lt. and Quartermaster of the 18th OVI and participated in all its battles of the Civil War. (Bowen)

+   259 M vii   Charles Henry GROSVENOR.

260 M viii   Capt. Edward GROSVENOR, b. 8 Jan 1836, Pomfret, Windham Co., CT; d. Sep 1864, Saundersville, GA.
Captain Edward Grosvenor was in the 2nd and 92nd OVI and in the battles of Chickamauga, Missionary Ridge, Dallas, Rockface Gap, Hoover's Gap and

Brown's Ferry. He died on Sherman's march at
Saundersville, Georgia. (Bowen)
+ 261 M ix Daniel Allan GROSVENOR

117 Godfrey Malbone GROSVENOR, b. 26 Sep 1773, Pomfret, Windham
Co., CT. Godfrey built the only store at Minot Corner, Maine.
In 1935 the building was still in use. (Bowen)
     Godfrey Malbone GROSVENOR m. (1) Mary TAINTOR 25 Aug
1798, Windham Co., CT.
     Godfrey m. (2) Deborah LOBDELL 25 May 1813. Deborah,
dau. of Isaac LOBDELL and Polly STETSON, b. 27 Sep 1786.

Children:
     262 M i   Seth GROSVENOR, b. 31 Mar 1815, Minot, ME.
     263 M ii   Thomas Peabody GROSVENOR, b. 27 Aug 1816, Minot,
                ME.
     264 F iii Mary Lobdell GROSVENOR, b. 1 Feb 1818, Minot, ME.
     265 F iv   Lucia Williams GROSVENOR, b. 28 Jun 1821, Minot,
                ME; d. 1877, Buffalo, NY.
     266 M v   William Pitt GROSVENOR, b. 10 Nov 1823, Minot, ME.
     267 M vi   Stetson Lobdell GROSVENOR, b. 30 May 1826, Minot,
                ME.

121 Abel Moore GROSVENOR, b. 23 Apr 1780, Pomfret, Windham Co.,
CT; d. 3 Jan 1813, Durham, Greene Co., NY; bur. Forest Lawn
Cem. Buffalo, NY.
     He m. Serene HEACOCK. Serene, dau. of Reuben HEACOCK and
Silence EASTON, b. 8 Aug 1784; d. 2 Apr 1867.

Children:
     268 M i   Abel Moore GROSVENOR, b. 10 Feb 1810; d. 6 Sep
                1849.
     269 M ii   Seth Heacock GROSVENOR, b. 24 Mar 1812; d. 13 May
                1864.

132 Peter Clark GROSVENOR, MD, b. 9 Aug 1771, Scituate, MA; d. 14
Dec. 1794, Fitzwilliam, NH.
     He m. Lucida BRIGHAM 5 May 1793, Fitzwilliam, NH.
Lucinda, dau. of Benjamin BRIGHAM and Lucy MORSE.

Child:
     270 M i   Ebenezer Clark GROSVENOR, MD, b. 21 Sep 1793,
                Fitzwilliam, NH; d. 1826, Darien, GA.

137 Charles GROSVENOR, b. 1 Oct 1775, Pomfret, CT; d. 9 Aug 1801.
     He m. Rebecca PLIMPTON.

Children:
+ 271 M i   Francis Dwight GROSVENOR.
   272 F ii   Harriet Plympton GROSVENOR, b. 1 Dec 1800.
              She m. Thomas Walter WARD 6 Apr 1825. Thomas, son
              of Thomas WARD and Elizabeth DENNY, b. 27 Nov 1798.

138 Payson GROSVENOR, b. 13 Dec 1776; d. 16 Oct 1861.
     He m. (1) Prudence GRAY 20 Apr 1803. Prudence, dau. of Thomas
     GRAY and Abigail WALES, b. 1780, Windham Co., CT; d. 17 Aug
     1835.

Children:
+   273 M i   Rev. Charles Payson GROSVENOR.
     274 M ii   Edward Wales GROSVENOR, b. 27 Jun 1806, Pomfret,
                Windham Co., CT; d. 9 Apr 1807, Pomfret, Windham
                Co., CT.
     275 F iii Zerviah GROSVENOR, b. 16 Jun 1809, Pomfret, Windham
                Co., CT; d. 8 Jan 1893.
                She m. Christopher COMSTOCK 6 Jan 1845.
     276 F iv   Mary Gray GROSVENOR, b. 15 Oct 1811, Pomfret,
                Windham Co., CT; d. 11 Jan 1889, Norfolk, NE.
                Mary m. Col. Charles MATHEWSON 23 Oct 1839.
                Charles, son of Darius MATHEWSON and Mary SMITH, b.
                24 Mar 1812, Brooklyn, CT; d. 10 May 1880, Norfolk,
                NE.
     277 F v   Elizabeth Hubbard GROSVENOR, b. 27 Feb 1815,
                Pomfret, Windham Co., CT; d. 21 Nov 1838, Pomfret,
                Windham Co., CT.
     278 M vi   Edward Dwight GROSVENOR, b. 31 May 1817, Pomfret,
                Windham Co., CT; d. 19 Aug 1841, Pomfret, Windham
                Co., CT.
     279 F vii Charlotte GROSVENOR, b. 28 Apr 1819, Pomfret,
                Windham Co., CT; d. 4 Jan 1820, Pomfret, Windham
                Co., CT.

     Payson GROSVENOR m. (2) Sophronia ABBOT. Sophronia, dau. of
     James ABBOT and Mehitable HOLT, b. 7 Dec 1791, Billerica, MA;
     d. 1 Dec 1869.

140 Oliver Clarke GROSVENOR, b. 9 Jun 1783, Pomfret, Windham Co.,
     CT; d. 8 Apr 1842, Rome, Oneida Co., NY
          He m. Harriet GRAY 10 Mar 1812. Harriet, dau. of Samuel
     GRAY and Charlotte ELDERKIN, b. 5 Feb 1790, Windham Co., CT;
     d. 13 Jan 1850, Rome, Oneida Co., NY.

Children:
+   280 M i   Oliver D. GROSVENOR.
     281 F ii   Charlotte Gray GROSVENOR, b. 28 May 1821; d. 25 Apr
                1898.
     282 M iii Francis Dwight GROSVENOR, b. 9 Jun 1833; d. 21 Jul
                1895.

141 Aaron GROSVENOR, MD, b. 27 Sep 1767, Pomfret, Windham Co., CT.
     He m. (1) Sally (_____).

Children:
     283 M i   John Milton GROSVENOR, b. 4 Apr 1793.
     284 M ii   Horace Hall GROSVENOR, b. 12 Apr 1795, Pelham, NH.
                He m. Julia Ann HASKINS 17 Dec 1844, Manchester,
                NH.

285 F iii Pauline Chipman GROSVENOR, b. 23 Jun 1797, Pelham,
            NH.   She m. Eben MARSH 6 Feb 1822, Pelham, NH.
            Eben, son of Ebenezer MARSH and Susanna CHASE, b. 6
            May 1796, W. Nottingham, NH.
286 F iv   Sally Hill GROSVENOR, b. 24 Apr 1799, Pelham, NH.
            She m. William M. BUTLER 14 Jan 1817, Pelham,NH.
287 M v   Aaron Putman GROSVENOR, b. 21 May 1801.
288 M vi   George Washington GROSVENOR, b. 11 Sep 1803.
289 M vii Benjamin French GROSVENOR, b. 18 Apr 1806, Pelham,
            MA.   He m. Mary Jane TITCOMB 13 Nov 1828, Pelham,
            NH.
290F viii Mary Gilmore GROSVENOR, b. 12 Aug 1809, Pelham, NH.
291 F ix   Martha Augusta GROSVENOR, b. 19 Mar 1814, Pelham,
            NH.
292 F x   Hannah Ariminta GROSVENOR, b. 15 Apr 1816, Pelham,
            NH.

148 David Augustus GROSVENOR, MD, b. 8 Dec 1784; d. 27 Sep 1889,
     Danvers, MA.
        He m. Sally GROSVENOR.   Sally, dau. of Ebenezer
     GROSVENOR, DD and Elizabeth CLARK, b. 29 Jul 1779, Scituate,
     MA; d. 14 Jul 1836.

Children:
     293 F i   Sally Eliza GROSVENOR, b. 2 Feb 1809, Manchester,
                MA.   She m. Rufus TAPLEY 18 Oct 1843, Reading, MA.
                Rufus, son of Amos TAPLEY and Hannah PRESTON, b. 16
                Oct 1800, Danvers, MA.
+   294 M ii   David Augustus GROSVENOR.
     295 M iii Ebenezer GROSVENOR, b. 21 Jun 1813, Manchester, MA;
                d. 19 Jan 1814, Manchester, MA.
+   296 M iv   Edwin Prescott GROSVENOR, MD.

149 Daniel Buckley GROSVENOR, b. 19 Aug 1777; d. 15 Jan 1821.
        He m. Lucy WILLISTON 23 May 1804.

Children:
+   297 M i   Joseph Williston GROSVENOR.
     298 F ii   Caroline Hall GROSVENOR, b. 6 Feb 1807, Brookfield,
                MA.   She m. Rev. Timothy Alden TAYLOR 2 Sep 1840.
                Timothy, son of Jeremiah TAYLOR and Martha (____),
                b. 7 Sep 1809, Hawley, MA; d. 2 Mar 1858.
     299 F iii Lucy Williston Ann GROSVENOR, b. 29 Jan 1809,
                Brookfield, MA.
                She m. Rev. John C. NICOLS 4 Dec 1834, Brookfield,
                MA.   John, son of Isaac NICOLS and Abigail CARTER,
                b. 17 Nov 1801, W. Brookfield, MA; d. 8 Jan 1868,
                Lyme, MA.
150 Col. David Hall GROSVENOR, b. 30 Nov 1779; d. 10 Aug 1842.
        He m. (1) Martha NEWTON 24 Apr 1804, Holden, MA.   Martha,
     dau of Silas NEWTON and Matilda GATES, b. 1782; d. 11 Apr
     1835.

FIFTH GENERATION

Children:
+   300 M i   David Rufus GROSVENOR.
+   301 M ii   Silas Newton GROSVENOR.
        302 F iii Lucy GROSVENOR, b. 20 Apr 1811, Petersham, MA. She
                   m. Rev. Allen WARREN 3 Mar 1841.
        303 M iv   Daniel GROSVENOR, b. 4 Dec 1813, Petersham, MA.
+   304 M v   Jonathan Prescott GROSVENOR.
        305 M vi   Lemuel Perkins GROSVENOR, b. 21 Sep 1823,
                   Petersham, MA; d. 30 Nov 1826.

        Col. David Hall GROSVENOR m. (2) Eliza BIGELOW 11 Jan 1837,
        Petersham, MA. Eliza, dau of Capt. Samuel BIGELOW and Betsey
        SANGER, b. 4 Apr 1792, Barre, MA; d. 7 Nov 1866.

151   Jonathan Prescott GROSVENOR, b. 30 Nov 1779
            He m. Bethiah AVERY 23 Apr 1804, Holden, MA. Bethiah,
        dau. of Joseph AVERY and Mary ALDEN, b. 13 Oct 1781, Holden,
        MA; d. 3 Jan 1833, Paxton, MA.

Children:
+   306 M i   Daniel Prescott GROSVENOR.
        307 F ii   Mary Avery GROSVENOR, b. 8 Aug 1806, Paxton, MA; d.
                   20 Jun 1811.
        308 M iii Joseph GROSVENOR, b. 22 Aug 1808, Paxton, MA; d. 30
                   May 1828.
        309 F iv   Lucy Bethiah GROSVENOR, b. 10 Mar 1810, Paxton, MA;
                   d. 17 Apr 1890, Worcester, MA.
        310 M v   David Hall GROSVENOR, b. 25 Feb 1812, Paxton, MA;
                   d. 23 Apr 1812.
        311 F vi   Catherine Ann GROSVENOR, b. 11 Mar 1813, Paxton,
                   MA; d. 28 May 1813, Paxton, MA.
        312 F vii Deborah Maria GROSVENOR, b. 21 Oct 1814, Paxton,
                   MA; d. 22 Dec 1814, Paxton, MA.
+   313 M viii Samuel Avery GROSVENOR.
        314 F ix   Harriet Newhall GROSVENOR, b. 5 May 1818, Paxton,
                   MA; d. 20 Jan 1904, Worcester, MA.
                   She m. Daniel Waldo KENT 9 Apr 1839. Daniel, son
                   of Daniel KENT and Ruth WATSON, b. 21 Jan 1810,
                   Leicester, MA; d. 11 Oct 1906.
                   Children: Lucy, Ruth, Prescott, Harriet, Daniel,
                   and Caroline.
        315 F x   Elizabeth Hall GROSVENOR, b. 29 Jun 1820, Paxton,
                   MA; d. 19 Jul 1906.
                   She m. Isaac Davis WHITE 18 May 1841. Isaac, son
                   of Aaron WHITE and Mary AVERY, b. 20 Mar 1806,
                   Boylston, MA; d. 10 Mar 1901, Brookline, MA.
        316 M xi   Jonathan Buckley GROSVENOR, b. 30 Apr 1822, Paxton,
                   MA; d. 6 Dec 1893, Worcester, MA.
                   He m. Sarah Jane LATIMER 8 Oct 1856, Hartford, CT.
                   Sarah, dau of Elisha LATIMER and Mary Ann GRISWOLD,
                   b. 1826, Wethersfield, CT; d. 10 Sep 1908,
                   Worcester, MA.

31

317 F xii Sarah Thaxter GROSVENOR, b. 9 Dec 1824, Paxton, MA;
d. 13 Feb 1895.
318M xiii Charles William GROSVENOR, b. 14 Feb 1827, Paxton,
MA.

153 Ebenezer Oliver GROSVENOR, b. 29 Oct 1783, Grafton, MA; d.
1870.
    He m. Mary Ann LIVERMORE 3 Jan 1814, Paxton, MA. Mary,
dau of Brad LIVERMORE and Mary FLINT, b. 13 Sep 1792, Paxton,
MA; d. 24 Sep 1849, Albion, MI.

Children:
    319 M i   Ira Rufus GROSVENOR, b. 18 Mar 1815, Paxton, MA.
    320 F ii   Caroline Maria GROSVENOR, b. 13 Aug 1818,
               Stillwater, NY.
               She m. Horace May HOVEY, MD 1 Apr 1837,
               Chittenango, NY. Horace, b. 22 Mar 1815, Mayville,
               NY; d. 20 Jan 1877, Albion, NY.
    321 M iii Ebenezer Oliver GROSVENOR, Jr. b. 20 Jan 1820,
               Stillwater; d. 26 Mar 1910, Jonesville, MI.
               Ebenezer was a State Senator of Michigan, Lawyer,
               President State Military Board and founder of
               Grosvenor Savings Bank of Jonesville. (Bowen)
               Ebenezer Oliver GROSVENOR, Jr. m. Sarah Ann
               CHAMPLIN 25 Feb 1844. Sarah, dau. of Elisha P.
               CHAMPLIN. Ebenezer and Sarah had three children:
               Ebenezer, Oliver and Charles.
    322 F iv   Mary Ann GROSVENOR, b. 18 Apr 1827, Chittenango,
               MI. She m. David PEABODY.
    323 F v   Adeline Selene GROSVENOR, b. 3 Mar 1829,
               Chittenango, MI. She m. Walter PEABODY.
    324 M vi   Daniel GROSVENOR, b. 8 Jun 1831, Chittenango, MI.
    325 F vii Harriet GROSVENOR, b. 12 Nov 1833, Chittenango, MI.

157 Rev. Cyrus Pitt GROSVENOR, b. 18 Oct 1792, Petersham, MA; d.
11 Feb 1879, Albion, MI.
    Rev. Cyrus graduated from Dartmouth in 1818; and received
his L.L.D. from Central College, New York in 1867. He was a
professor and president of Central College 1849-1865. Rev.
Cyrus edited the "Christian Reflector", an anti-slavery
Baptist paper founded in 1838.   (Bowen)
    Rev. Cyrus Pitt GROSVENOR m. Sarah W. WARNER.

Child:
    326 M i   Cyrus Pitt Daniel GROSVENOR, b. 1824; d. 5 Jun
               1849, Southbridge, MA.
               He m. Arinda AMMIDOWN. Arinda, dau. of Adolphus
               AMMIDOWN and Sally Maria VINTON, b. 14 Dec 1828,
               Southbridge, MA; d. Feb 1889.

159   Lemuel Putman GROSVENOR, b. 26 Oct 1784, Pomfret, Windham Co., CT; d. 19 Jan 1858. Lemuel was a Deacon in Park St. Church, Boston. He was interested in the East India trade and visited China. (Bowen)
      Lemuel Putman GROSVENOR m. Clarissa DOWNS. Clarissa, b. 1786; d. 9 May 1857, Pomfret, Windham Co., CT

Children:
  327 F i   Charlotte Otis GROSVENOR, b. 30 Jan 1810, Boston, MA; d. 22 Oct 1847, Calais, ME.
      She m. James Shepard PIKE 21 Sep 1837, Boston, MA. James, son of William PIKE and Hannah SHEPARD, b. 8 Sep 1811, Calais, ME; d. 29 Nov 1882, Boston, MA.
  328 F ii   Louisa GROSVENOR, b. 1815, Boston, MA; d. 10 Aug 1869, Pomfret, Windham Co., CT.
  329 M iii   Rev. Lemuel GROSVENOR, b. 27 Apr 1814, Boston, MA; d. 8 Aug 1870, London, ENG.
      He m. (1) Hannah PEARCE 21 Oct 1845.
      He m. (2) Grace DUGANNE 27 Apr 1866, Boston MA.
  330 F iv   Clara GROSVENOR, b. 6 Jul 1817, Boston, MA; d. 10 Jan 1890.
      She m. Charles Stockbridge THOMPSON 7 Aug 1844, Pomfret, Windham Co., CT. Charles, son of Ebenezer THOMPSON and Ruth STOCKBRIDGE, b. 2 Jun 1812, Pomfret, Windham Co., CT; d. 10 Apr 1891, Pomfret, Windham Co., CT.
      Children: Ebenezer and Charles.
  331 F v   Caroline Downs GROSVENOR, b. 28 Nov 1823, Boston MA; d. 2 Jan 1896.
      She m. Thomas Wells PERRY, MD. Thomas, b. 27 Oct 1823, Hopkinton, RI; d. 5 Jan 1894, Providence RI.
      Children: Lemuel and Roswell.

180   Nathan Ebenezer GROSVENOR, b. 24 Feb 1794, Pomfret, Windham Co., CT; d. 27 May 1877, Claridon, Geauga Co., OH.
      Nathan was a cabinet maker with a business in Mansfield CT. He pioneered to Geauga Co., OH. He was active in the Congregational Church and his children were baptized there. (Jeanette Grosvenor)
      Nathan Ebenezer GROSVENOR m. Laura FULLER 15 Oct 1827. Laura, b. 13 May 1807, Mansfield, CT; d. 12 Nov 1882, Portage Co., OH.

Children:
  332 M i   George Adams GROSVENOR, b. 30 Aug 1828, Mansfield, CT; d. 22 Oct 1832, Mansfield, CT.
+ 333 M ii   Edward Nathan GROSVENOR.
+ 334 M iii   John Flavell GROSVENOR.
  335 F iv   Mary Eliza GROSVENOR, b. 28 Oct 1834, Mansfield.
  336 F v   Lucy Fitch GROSVENOR, b. 7 Feb 1837, Washington, Litchfield Co., CT.
  337 F vi   Emily Fuller GROSVENOR, b. 21 Nov 1839, Mansfield, CT.

338 F vii Olive Judd GROSVENOR, b. 21 Jun 1842
339F viii Maria Williams GROSVENOR, b. 1 Oct 1845, Mansfield, CT.

183 Rev. Mason GROSVENOR, b. 13 Sep 1800, Pomfret, Windham Co., CT; d. 22 Mar 1886, Englewood, NJ.
Mason was a Clergyman and Educator. He graduated from Yale in 1827 and received his AM and DD degrees. He served as a Congregationalist Pastor for ten years in Connecticut and Ohio. He founded a female Seminary at Hudson, Ohio. He held the chair of Moral Philosophy at the University of Illinois of which he was a founder. He retired in 1880 and lived with his son Col. William Mason Grosvenor, until his death. (Cyclopedia, Vol 20)
Rev. Mason GROSVENOR m. (1) Esther Delia SCARBOROUGH 18 Jun 1833, Brooklyn, CT. Esther, dau. of Joel SCARBOROUGH and Lucretia SMITH, b. 10 Aug 1812, Brooklyn, CT; d. 6 Apr 1846.

Children:
+ 340 M i Col. William Mason GROSVENOR.
341 M ii Charles Scarborough GROSVENOR.
342 M iii Charles Henry GROSVENOR, b. 18 Apr 1841.
343 F iv Mary Lucretia GROSVENOR.

Rev. Mason GROSVENOR m. (2) Lucy TAPPAN 25 Apr 1849. Lucy, d. 1883.

184 Rev. David Adams GROSVENOR, b. 10 Jul 1802, Craftsbury, VT; d. 11 Aug 1866, Cincinnatti, OH.
He m. Sarah WHITNEY 5 May 1835, Princeton, MA. Sarah, dau. of Capt. Andrew WHITNEY and Lucy MILES, b. 4 Jun 1803, Princeton, MA; d. 4 Feb 1894, Weston, OH.

Child:
344 F i Ellen Louise GROSVENOR, d. Jul 1842; bur. Uxbridge, MA.

186 Willard GROSVENOR, b. 28 Dec 1765, Pomfret, Windham Co., CT; d. 18 Aug 1837, Feeding Hills, MA.
He m. Abigail SHERMAN 12 Feb 1789, Brimfield, MA. Abigail, dau. of John SHERMAN and Lucy HOAR, b. 3 Aug 1769, Brimfield, MA; d. 11 Jun 1840, Feeding Hills, MA.

Children:
+ 345 M i Gordon GROSVENOR.
346 M ii Pearley GROSVENOR, b. 15 May 1791, Suffield, CT; d. VA.
347 M iii Persis GROSVENOR, b. 5 Apr 1793, Suffield, CT; d. Feeding Hills, MA.
348 F iv Lucy GROSVENOR, b. 9 Aug 1795, Suffield, CT.
349 F v Polly GROSVENOR, b. 4 May 1797, Suffield, CT.
She m. George KING 5 May 1818, Battleboro, VT
350 M vi William GROSVENOR, b. 30 Jun 1799, Suffield, CT.

351 M vii   Thomas GROSVENOR, b. 10 Apr 1801, Suffield, CT; d. 20 Sep 1878.

352F viii   Clarissa GROSVENOR, b. 23 Oct 1803, Suffield, CT; She m. Henry PORTER 20 Jul 1823.

353 F ix   Eliza GROSVENOR, b. 7 Aug 1805, Suffield, CT; d. 1 Sep 1888, Warrensburg, IL.

354 F x   Abigail GROSVENOR, b. 17 Jun 1807, Suffield, CT.

355 M xi   John GROSVENOR, b. 31 Oct 1809, Suffield, Ct; d. 18 Oct 1834, Feeding Hills, MA.

356 M xii   Sherman GROSVENOR, b. 27 Sep 1811, Suffield, CT. Sherman settled in Louisiana. (Bailey)

189   Moses GROSVENOR Jr, b. 9 Nov 1773, Pomfret, Windham Co., CT. He m. Mary SYKES 20 Aug 1796, Wilbraham, MA. Mary, dau of Col. R. SYKES.

Children:

357 M i   John GROSVENOR, b. 3 Feb 1796, Wilbraham, MA.

358 F ii   Mary GROSVENOR, b. 14 Jan 1800, Wilbraham, MA; d. 25 Sep 1864.
            She m. Edward Dillingham BANGS 12 Apr 1824. Edward, son of Edward BANGS and Hannah LYNDE, b. 24 Aug 1790.

190   Amasa GROSVENOR, b. 27 Dec 1776, Pomfret, Windham Co., CT; d. 4 Feb 1843, Carlisle, NY.
       He m. Phoebe KENYON. Phoebe, dau. of Oliver KENYON and Sarah SWEET, b. 1782, Richmond, RI; d. 5 Mar 1843, Grosvenor Corners, NY

Children:

+   359 M i   Chauncey GROSVENOR.
+   360 M ii   George GROSVENOR.
+   361 M iii   Niram GROSVENOR.
     362 M iv   Alvin Sharpe GROSVENOR, b. 6 Jun 1806, Grosvenor Corners, NY; d. 4 Dec 1874, Council Bluffs, IA.
                 He m. Ellen OTIS Feb 1834. Ellen, b., Charleston, SC.
     363 F v   Amelia GROSVENOR, b. 10 Mar 1808.
+   364 M vi   Calvin GROSVENOR.
     365 F vii   Sarah GROSVENOR, b. 4 Feb 1815, Grosvenor Corners, NY. She m. Jonathan GUFFIN. Jonathan, son of Andrew GUFFIN and Hannah YOUNG, b. 15 Sep 1814; d. 11 Jan 1892. Child: Alvin
     366F viii   Nancy GROSVENOR, b. 31 Aug 1816, Grosvenor Corners, NY; d. Council Bluffs, IA.
                 Nancy and Levi are listed in the 1880 Federal Census of Council Bluffs, Iowa. (Bailey)
                 Nancy GROSVENOR m. Levi GUNN 19 Dec 1838. Levi, son of Joseph GUNN and Annie SWEETZER, b. 6 May 1813, Montaque, MA.
                 Children: Charles, Josephine, Sarah, Austin, Fanny, Austin and Walton.

```
+    367 M  ix   Rev. Parley GROSVENOR
     368 M  x    Walton GROSVENOR, b. 25 Jun 1824, Grosvenor
                 Corners, NY; d. 10 May 1856, Grosvenor Corners, NY.
                 Walton died unmarried. (Bailey)
     369 M  xi   Dorcas GROSVENOR, b. 5 May 1827, Grosvenor Corners,
                 NY; d. Grosvenor Corners, NY.  Dorcas died
                 unmarried. (Bailey)
```

194   Ebenezer Griffin GROSVENOR, b. 15 Feb 1781, Pomfret, Windham
      Co., CT.
           He m. (1) Martha WRIGHT 23 May 1805, Lanesboro, MA.
      Martha d. 18 Feb 1825, Lebanon, NY.

Children:
```
     370 M  i    Chandler GROSVENOR, b. 1806, Lebanon, Madison Co.,
                 NY; d. Jan 1829.
+    371 M  ii   Augustus Livingston GROSVENOR.
+    372 M  iii  Sydney Algernon GROSVENOR.
     373 F  iv   Olive Millicent GROSVENOR, b. 1811, Lebanon,
                 Madison Co., NY; d. 28 Apr 1859.
                 She m. Chandler HOPPIN Sep 1832.  Chandler, d. 28
                 Apr 1839.
     374 M  v    Chandler Bradley GROSVENOR, b. Apr 1830, Lebanon,
                 Madison Co., NY; d. Aug 1833.
     375 F  vi   Harriet Elizabeth GROSVENOR, b. 26 Jul 1832,
                 Lebanon, Madison Co., NY; d. 7 Feb 1895.
                 She m. Edwin G. GILBERT 10 Jan 1872.  Edwin, son of
                 Vine B. GILBERT and Louisa GLEASON, b. 2 Aug 1834,
                 Lebanon, Madison Co., NY; d. 4 Jan 1902.
     376 F  vii  Mary Adelia GROSVENOR, b. 18 Mar 1835, Lebanon,
                 Madison Co., NY; d. 4 Oct 1899.
                 She m. Warren Mason LASELLE 8 Mar 1854.  Warren,
                 son of Mason LASELLE and Dorcas CONANT, b. 7 Apr
                 1833, Lebanon, NY; d. 11 Jun 1914.
                 Children:  Adelaide, Adelia, Frank and Elizabeth.
```

      Ebenezer Griffin GROSVENOR m. (2) Elizabeth ANDRUS Aug 1826.
      Elizabeth, b. 13 Dec 1794; d. 28 Mar 1838.

195   Vine GROSVENOR, b. 17 May 1783, Pomfret, Windham Co., CT.
           He m. Laura MERRILL 6 May 1805, Pittsfield, MA. Laura,
      dau. of Hosea MERRILL, b. 23 May 1786, Pittsfield, MA.

Children:
```
     377 F  i    Lucy GROSVENOR, b. 1806, Lanesboro, MA; d. 16 May
                 1810
     378 M  ii   George GROSVENOR, b. Jan 1813, Lanesboro, MA; d. 14
                 Apr 1814.
```

204   John Williams GROSVENOR, b. 8 Oct 1806, Pomfret, Windham Co.,
      CT. He m. Phebe G. SPALDING 26 Jun 1828. Phebe, dau. of
      Charles SPALDING, b. 1 Nov 1814; d. 9 Apr 1898.

FIFTH GENERATION

Children:
+   379 M   i   Charles Williams GROSVENOR.
+   380 M   ii   Benjamin Hutchins GROSVENOR.
    381 F   iii Hannah GROSVENOR, b. 12 Mar 1845, Pomfret, Windham
                 Co., CT; d. 20 Jun 1869.
    382 F   iv   Julia GROSVENOR, b. 25 Jan 1847, Pomfret, Windham
                 Co., CT; d. 27 Feb 1871.

210 Capt Thomas GROSVENOR, b. 4 Apr 1809, Pomfret, Windham Co.,
    CT; d. 28 Nov 1882, Pomfret, Windham Co., CT.
        He m. Ruth Spalding HUTCHINS 6 Mar 1837. Ruth, b. 1 Oct
    1811, Killingly, MA; d. 10 Dec 1877.

Children:
    383 M   i   Thomas Perrin GROSVENOR, b. 13 Oct 1838, Pomfret,
                 Windham Co., CT; d. 1852.
    384 F   ii   Mary Ann GROSVENOR, b. 19 Jun 1842, Pomfret,
                 Windham Co., CT; d. 4 May 1911.
                 She m. Samuel Henry SMITH 2 May 1866, Pomfret,
                 Windham Co., CT. Samuel, son of Abner SMITH and
                 Alma LILY, b. 1844, Ashford; d. 22 Jan 1890.
                 Children: Clarence, Ada, Harry, Mary, Alma and
                 Chester.
+   385 M   iii Edward Hutchins GROSVENOR.

215 Payson Jasper GROSVENOR, b. 14 Jan 1790, Pomfret, Windham Co.,
    CT; d. 25 Mar 1832.
        He m. Nancy C. GORDON 15 Sep 1815. Nancy, dau. of
    Alexander GORDON and Hattie HUNTINGTON, b. 2 Jan 1792; d. 25
    Dec 1845.

Children:
    386 F   i   Frances H. GROSVENOR, b. 29 Jun 1816. She m. E. M.
                 BATES 13 Sep 1837.
    387 F   ii   Eliza GROSVENOR, b. 23 Feb 1818, Pomfret, Windham
                 Co., CT.
    388 F   iii Charlotte Elderkin GROSVENOR, b. 27 May 1820,
                 Pomfret, Windham Co., CT.
    389 M   iv   Alexander GROSVENOR, b. 18 Jan 1829, Pomfret,
                 Windham Co., CT; d. 28 Feb 1848.
    390 M   v   Frederick William GROSVENOR, b. 3 Dec 1830,
                 Pomfret, Windham Co., CT; d. 1 Feb 1833.

217 Jasper GROSVENOR, b. 11 Oct 1794, Pomfret, Windham Co., CT; d.
    8 May 1857, New York, NY.
        He m. Matilda Agnes SIDELL. Matilda, dau. of John
    SIDELL, b. 9 Jan 1800, New York, NY; d. 20 Jan 1885.

Child:
    391 F   i   Charlotte Matilda GROSVENOR, b. 31 Mar 1839, New
                 York, NY; d. 3 Mar 1902, San Luis Obispo, CA.

She m. Frederick GOODRIDGE 22 Jun 1864. Frederick, son of Samuel GOODRIDGE and Lydia READ, b. 11 Jan 1836, Hartford, CT; d. 27 Apr 1897.
Children: Jasper, Matilda, Charlotte, Caroline, and Frederic.

220   Charles Ingalls GROSVENOR, b. 18 Feb 1802, Pomfret, Windham Co., CT; d. 28 Jan 1864.
      He m. (1) Angeline MOSLEY 16 Oct 1827, Mansfield, CT. Angeline, dau. of Flaviel MOSLEY and Jane DORRANCE, b. 10 Aug 1804, Hampton, CT; d. 13 Feb 1832, Hampton, CT.

Child:
      392 F i   Maria Jane GROSVENOR, b. 15 Feb 1829, Abington, MA; d. 24 Aug 1885.
                 She m. Samuel Walter LYON 28 Sep 1851. Samuel, son of Samuel H. LYON and Maria WARNER, b. 20 Dec 1822, Pomfret, Windham Co., CT; d. 31 May 1880.

Charles m. (2) Euretta Catherine GORDON 13 Mar 1833. Euretta, dau. of John GORDON and Lucy MOORE, b. 10 Jan 1803, Canterbury, CT; d. 2 Apr 1887.

225   William GROSVENOR, MD, b. 30 Apr 1810, Killingly, CT; d. 12 Aug 1888, Maplewood, NH.
      Dr. William studied at Pennsylvania Hospital and had his practice at Killingly with his father Dr. Robert. He moved to Providence in 1837 and became senior partner of the firm of Grosvenor and Chase, wholesale druggists. He and his wife inherited a mill at Thompson and its name was changed to Grosvenor-Dale. William became head of the largest cotton textile mill in Connecticut. (Bowen)
      William GROSVENOR, MD m. Rosa Ann MASON 22 Aug 1837. Rosa, dau. of James MASON and Alice BROWN, b. 10 Nov 1817, Providence, RI; d. 12 Apr 1872.

Children:
+   393 M i   William GROSVENOR.
      394 M ii   James Brown Mason GROSVENOR, b. 12 Feb 1840, Providence, RI; d. 25 Sep 1905, New York, NY.
                 James was in the Civil War. He was in the Providence office of Grosvenor-Dale Co., and founded the house of Grosvenor and Co., New York. He was president of Grosvenor-Dale Co. and a director of several companies. (Bowen)
                 James Brown Mason GROSVENOR m. Minna Jean LUDELING 1896. Minna, dau of John T. LUDELING.
      395 F iii Amara Mason GROSVENOR.
      396 F iv   Alice Mason GROSVENOR, b. 19 Oct 1843, Providence, RI; d. 14 Jan 1886.
                 She m. John J. MASON, MD 26 Jun 1867. John, son of W. H. MASON.

FIFTH GENERATION

397 M v   Robert GROSVENOR, b. 2 Nov 1847, Providence, RI; d. 19 Jul 1879, Providence, RI.
Robert was associated with his brother William in the management of the Providence office of the Grosvenor-Dale Co. (Bowen)
Robert GROSVENOR m. Mary WRIGHT Oct 1875. Mary, b. Baltimore, MD.

398 F vi   Eliza Howe GROSVENOR, b. 12 Feb 1849, Providence, RI; d. 2 May 1853.

399 F vii   Rosa Ann GROSVENOR, b. 2 Jul 1855, Providence, RI. Rosa Ann lived at 340 Park Ave (living 1934) and had a summer home at Newport, RI. She was a member of the Colony Club of New York and the National Society of the Colonial Dames. (Bowen)

228   Robert Howe GROSVENOR, b. 26 Apr 1796, Killingly, MA; d. 8 Sep 1829.
He m. Lucretia HARTSHORN 8 Jan 1824. Lucretia, dau of Samuel HARTSHORN, MD and Sarah TROWBRIDGE, b. 1797, Pomfret, Windham Co., CT; d. 7 Jan 1841.

Child:
+   400 M i   Samuel Howe GROSVENOR.

SIXTH GENERATION

232   Julius Thornton GROSVENOR, b. 8 Sep 1826, Troy, Miami Co., OH; d. 23 Feb 1864, Union City, IN; bur., Rose Hill Cem., Troy, OH. Julius was a druggist and the manager of his father's store as Daniel was a store owner, an attorney, and constantly engaged in civic activity. Julius' children are registered in the records of the Troy Baptist Church.
During the Civil War Daniel purchased a drugstore in Union City, Indiana, and sent Julius to manage it and Chauncey to clerk. Julius died in February 1864 and Chauncey was at his bedside with his family. Julius was buried at Rose Hill Cemetery in a funeral under the auspices of the I.O.O.F. of which he was a member. His family returned to Troy. (Abbey Grosvenor)
Julius Thornton GROSVENOR m. Susan Ellen BAER 27 May 1851. Susan, dau. of William BAER and Elizabeth FAUBLE, b. 1828; d. 31 Jan 1909, Richmond, IN; bur. Rose Hill Cem. Troy, OH.

Children:
+   401 M i   Albert Barber GROSVENOR, DDS.
+   402 M ii   William Daniel GROSVENOR.
+   403 M iii Edward Thornton GROSVENOR, MD.
+   404 M iv   Elmer Baer GROSVENOR, MD.

235   Mary Frances GROSVENOR, b. 17 May 1833, Troy, Miami, OH; d. 10 Dec 1921, Clarinda, IA; bur., Clarinda, IA.

She m. Ansel Bishop CRAMER 15 Feb 1852. Ansel, son of Russel CRAMER and Sarah SMITH, b. 23 Jan 1828, Vergennes, VT; d. 9 Dec 1891, Clarinda, IA.

Children:
    405 M i   Otis Ansel CRAMER, b. 8 Jul 1854, Rock Co., WI. He m. Annie Eliza POAGE 20 Jun 1888. Annie, dau. of Rev. Josiah B. POAGE and Frances Ann ARBUCKLE, b. 20 Dec 1856, Ashley, MO.
    406 F ii   Carrie Frances CRAMER, b. 23 Jul 1856, Rock Co., WI. She m. William Woods BISBY 8 Nov 1876. William, b. 8 Nov 1852, Clarksville, PA.
    407 F iii Florence Aurelia CRAMER, b. 21 May 1860, Clarinda, IA; d. 15 Jun 1862.
    408 M iv   Fred Henry CRAMER, b. 24 May 1863, Clarinda, IA; d. 8 Nov 1865.
    409 F v   Mabel Irene CRAMER, b. 8 Jan 1865, Clarinda, IA. She m. Isaac Leslie MAXWELL 19 Dec 1893. Isaac, son of Adam MAXWELL and Maria YETTER, b. 30 Jan 1862, Butler, PA.
    410 F vi   Nellie Gertrude CRAMER, b. 2 Oct 1872, Clarinda, IA. She m. Clark RAY 20 Oct 1896. Clark, son of Matthew S. RAY and Margaret C. BUTTERFIELD, b. 10 Jul 1872, Clarinda, IA.
    411 M vii Walter Clarence CRAMER, b. 16 Feb 1874, Clarinda, IA. He m. Maud THOMPSON 1 Jun 1899. Maud, dau of Isaac Milton THOMPSON and Anna Eliza VINSTOT, b. 2 Oct 1877, Clarinda, IA.

236 Augustus Daniel GROSVENOR, b. 19 Jun 1837, Troy, Miami, OH; d. 28 Jul 1909, Clarinda, Page Co., IA; bur. Clarinda, IA.
    Augustus joined the 11th regiment of the Ohio Volunteer Infantry at the time of its formation in Troy in 1861. A ribbon from an 1895 reunion shows that by 1864 the regiment had fought in 15 battles including Bull Run, Antietam, Chickamaugua, Lookout Mountain, and Rocky Face Ridge. In about March 1864 Gus was severly wounded in the battle of Rocky Face Ridge. He recovered and in the winter of 1864-65 enlisted in the 110th regiment and served until the end of the war. He and Chauncey met at Washington DC at the close of the war. Gus married Hester Culbertson in Troy in 1866 and moved to Clarinda, Iowa, where he lived for the rest of his life. An 1896 photo in Chauncey's album shows Gus and Hester in front of their Clarinda home. (Chauncey) (Grosvenor Documents)
    Augustus Daniel GROSVENOR m. Charlotte Hester CULBERTSON 22 Mar 1866. Charlotte, dau. of Charles H. CULBERTSON and Elizabeth STEWART, d. 15 Nov 1909, Clorinda, Page Co., IA.

Child:
    412 F i   Elizabeth GROSVENOR m. (_____) HILL.

238 Chauncey Frederick GROSVENOR, b. 15 Oct 1845, Troy, Miami Co.,
     OH; d. 22 Nov 1902, Troy, Miami Co., OH; bur. Riverside Cem.
     Troy, OH.
          In May 1864 Chauncey joined the 147th regiment OVI for
     three months service. He was sent to Fort Marcy at Washington
     DC where he served as Fort Guard and on pickett duty. In July
     he saw Early's Confederate Veterans charge the Union lines in
     an effort to take Washington. Veterans of the Union Sixth
     Corp piled up the Confederates with rifle shots and saved the
     city.
          After his three months service Chaucey joined the 17th
     regiment of the OVI and was sent to Chattanooga, TN on top of
     a freight car, as the cars were full of supplies. At
     Chattanooga he was placed in squalid quarters and came down
     with inflammatory rheumatism. He was in the hospital when
     General Sherman's troops began their march to Atlanta, and
     when well, he was sent by train and boat to Savannah, GA to
     rejoin Sherman's army. There he was placed in the fife and
     drum corp, as a fifer. The Corp played reveille each day and
     a few tunes at the start of each march. On the march north
     Chauncey carried his fife and a skillet that he had
     "captured." His baggage and tentage were carried by a small
     donkey that was assigned to the corps. The troops marched
     through rain, mud and occasional bullets to Virginia, arriving
     there shortly after the surrender of Richmond. A few days
     later the men were drawn up in ranks and read a message
     detailing the assassination of President Lincoln. A deathly
     silence followed this announcement, men stood as if paralyzed
     and many wept. In May 1865 Chauncey took part in the grand
     review at Washington and received his discharge.
          The Census of 1870 shows that Chauncey was working at his
     chosen vocation of law. He specialized in pension cases. In
     1876 he joined his father-in-law, William Browne Locke, in
     publishing the Troy Free Press. The paper failed in 1877. In
     1880 Chauncey was appointed official stenographer of Miami
     County, a position that he held for the rest of his life.
          In 1876 he joined the Ohio National Guard, eventually
     rising to the position of Captain. He served in the railroad
     riots of 1877 and the Cincinnatti riot a few years later
     during his ten years service in the Guard. He was also a
     member of the A.H.Coleman Post of the GAR and filled nearly
     every chair in the Post, including that of Commander. In 1885
     Chauncey and Mary joined the Troy First Methodist Church.
     Chauncey served five years on the official board.
          Chauncey's recreation included acting in plays, fishing,
     and photography. In 1893 he spent two weeks on a fishing boat
     off the Florida coast. He filled a photo album with his own
     snapshots and left another sixty studio pictures covering the
     years 1863 to 1901. In 1901 he finished writing his Civil War
     experiences. This was published in 1994. (See list of
     sources)
          On November 11, 1902 Chauncey suffered a fatal heart
     attack while bailing out his fishing boat. His funeral was

held in the Methodist Church with the GAR in charge, the Bar Association attending as a body. He was buried at Rose Hill Cemetery near his parents, his sisters Vinnie and Juliet and his brother Julius. (Grosvenor Documents) (Chauncey Grosvenor)

Chauncey Frederick GROSVENOR m. Mary Florence LOCKE 4 May 1871, Troy, OH. Mary, dau. of William Browne LOCKE and Angeline Elmyra FIDLER, b. 2 Sep 1849, Troy, Miami Co., OH; d. Feb 1920, Troy, Miami Co., Oh; bur. 29 Feb 1920, Riverside Cem., Troy, Miami Co., OH.

Mary Florence graduated from Troy High School in 1868, a member of a class of nine. The Federal Census of 1870 lists her as a school teacher. Early tintype photos show her to be a pretty woman. She helped Chauncey in the years before he had a typewriter at the office by typing the notes that he took as Court Stenographer.

Their daughters became of courting age during the 1890's when disapproval of dancing and card playing had greatly declined in Troy and few ministers denounced these twin evils from the pulpit. This viewpoint had very little effect on Mary Florence who thought that any young man who danced, played cards, or smoked was not good enough for her daughters. She also believed that the oldest daughter should marry first. Clifford did not marry and all three stayed single, lived together, and taught school.

Mary Florence understood the importance of family history. After Chauncey's death she saved the Locke and Grosvenor Bible records, photos and documents dating as far back as 1818. She loaned the bible pages to Abbey Johnson Grosvenor to enable her to write the "Grosvenor Pedigree" for the Grosvenor Library of Buffalo, N.Y.

Mary Florence appeared to relax and enjoy life more after she became a grandmother. She posed happily in a 1916 picture with her mother, son, and grandson. This is the only picture in our collection in which she is smiling. She died of cancer in Feb 1920 and was buried in Riverside Cemetery on Feb 29. Chauncey's casket was moved from Rose Hill to lie beside hers. (RBG)

Children:
    413 F i   Clifford Locke GROSVENOR, b. 12 Oct 1874, Troy, OH; d. 27 Feb 1960, Troy, OH; bur. Riverside Cem., Troy, OH.

Clifford graduated from Troy High School in June 1894 as a member of a class of nine. She studied at a Normal School and in June 1895 received a Teaching Certificate. She taught school in Troy until 1923 when she moved with her sisters to Cuyahoga Falls, Ohio, where she became Principal of East School. She retired in 1940 and returned to Troy. She did not marry and lived with her two single sisters. (RBG)

414 F ii Frances Elmira GROSVENOR, b. 3 Feb 1876, Troy, OH;
d. 18 Apr 1940, Cuyahoga Falls, Summit Co., OH;
bur. Riverside Cem., Troy, OH.
Frances taught school in Troy until 1907 when she
went to San Diego, CA to teach. She had a hobby of
photography and filled an album with pictures of
California and other Western States. She returned
to Troy to teach and then in 1923 went to Akron, OH
to teach elementary school. She suffered from
heart trouble, but continued teaching almost until
her death in April 1940.

415 F iii Carrie Corinne GROSVENOR, b. 26 May 1877, Troy, OH;
d. Apr 1948, Troy, OH; bur. 22 Apr 1948, Riverside
Cem., Troy, OH.
Corinne taught at Troy and moved to Cuyahoga Falls
with her sisters in 1923. She became Principal of
Crawford School. She was a pioneer at bird
watching with binoculars. I have a 1907 photograph
of her using binoculars. She retired from teaching
in 1940 and returned to Troy. In 1947 she had
serious heart trouble and was confined to her room
for six months prior to her death. I had the good
fortune to be a student in her Fifth Grade class as
she was an excellent teacher. (RBG)

+   416 M iv Fred Browne GROSVENOR, MD.

239 Reuben Safford GROSVENOR m. Elizabeth Helen ALCOTT.
Elizabeth, b. 21 Nov 1821, Hoboken, NY; d. Jun 1888.

Child:
+   417 M i Walter Reed GROSVENOR.

241 Nathan GROSVENOR, b. 1794; d. 15 Mar 1842.
Nathan was blind at death and left a personal estate of
$200.75. This included a note from John GROSVENOR for $77.00.
(Suzanne Soltess)
Nathan GROSVENOR m. Nancy BOOKTUS bef 1825. Nancy, b.
abt 1798, Reading, PA; d. 23 Mar 1862.

Children:
+   418 M i Napoleon P. GROSVENOR.
     419 F ii Josephine GROSVENOR, b. 6 May 1829; d. 31 May 1900.
She m. Robert Kimball RUSSELL 22 Jun 1848. Robert,
b. 23 Jun 1822.
Children: Frank, Ida, Nellie and Jettye.
     420 M iii Israel Curtis GROSVENOR, b. 9 Jun 1831; d. 28 Feb
1890. He m. Martha HOXIE 1854.
     421 F iv Lucia GROSVENOR, b. 1832; d. 1917, Youngsville, PA.
She m. William H. JACKSON, 27 Mar 1852.
     422 F v Lorinda Eunice GROSVENOR m. John WEDGE.
     423 F vi Sarah Jane GROSVENOR m. Everand H. KING.
     424 F vii Lucinda GROSVENOR m. John EBBERT.

425F viii Lutitia GROSVENOR.
426 F IX Eliza Ann GROSVENOR m. Lewis D. SMITH.

246 Thomas GROSVENOR, b. 31 Aug 1825, Pomfret, Windham Co., CT; d. 14 Apr 1862, Huntsville, AL.
    Thomas was in the 18th OVI in the Civil War and died of brain fever. (Bowen)
    Thomas GROSVENOR m. Mary Carpenter WYATT 1 Nov 1847. Mary, dau. of John WYATT and Emily CARPENTER, b. 19 Mar 1828, Ames, Athens Co., OH; d. 5 Jan 1902.

Children:
    427 F i   Henrietta GROSVENOR, b. 1 Jul 1848, Canaan, Athens Co., OH; d. 12 Jan 1884.
    428 M ii   William Parker GROSVENOR, b. 6 Jun 1850, Canaan, Athens Co., OH; d. 10 Aug 1863.
    429 F iii Eliza GROSVENOR, b. 14 Nov 1852, Canaan, Athens Co., OH. She m. George YOUNGER.
    430 F iv   Anna GROSVENOR, b. 5 Sep 1855, Canaan, Athens Co., OH. She m. John JOHNSON.
    431 F v   Hattie GROSVENOR, b. 22 Jun 1857, Canaan, Athens Co., OH; d. 20 Dec 1931. She m. Charles W. RANDOLPH.
 + 432 M vi   John Harvey GROSVENOR.
    433 F vii Sarah GROSVENOR, b. 13 Dec 1861, Canaan, Athens Co., OH. She m. Oliver HILL 18 Nov 1893. Oliver, son of Daniel HILL and Flora LEWIS, b. 30 Apr 1867, Athens, OH.

247 Capt. Samuel Lee GROSVENOR, b. 16 Jul 1827; d. 30 Jan 1918.
    Samuel was a Lieutenant in Co., B 36th Ohio Regiment in the Civil War. He was in the battles of Second Bull Run, South Mountain, Antietam, Lexington, and Lynchburg. He led his company as Captain at Chickamauga and was mustered out in 1865. (Bowen)
    Capt. Samuel Lee GROSVENOR m. (1) Mary Cutler DUNBAR 7 Jan 1848. Mary, dau. of Stephen DUNBAR and Lucy CUTLER, b. 14 Jun 1829, Amherst, MA; d. 3 Feb 1857, Bartlett, OH.

Children:
    434 F.i   Alice GROSVENOR, b. 7 Apr 1850.
               She m. Orville Orlando ELLENWOOD 14 Sep 1879. Orville, son of Sylvester ELLENWOOD and Lucy DELANO, b. 11 Feb 1853, Dunham, Washington Co., OH; d. 10 Oct 1913.
    435 F ii   Lucy Adelia GROSVENOR, b. 22 Mar 1852, Rome, Athens Co., OH. She m. Theodore BRACKEN 25 Nov 1874. Theodore, son of Newton BRACKEN and Pamela CRAIG, b. 23 Oct 1849, Porterville, PA; d. 10 Jun 1914.
    436 M iii Lee Cutler GROSVENOR, b. 27 Jan 1857, Rome, Athens Co., OH; d. 21 Dec 1871.

SIXTH GENERATION

Samuel m. (2) Thirza A. COOK 16 Dec 1860. Thirza, dau. of
Orange E. COOK and Amanda E. CHAMBERLIN, b. 29 Nov 1839,
Palmer, Washington Co., OH; d. 2 Jan 1898.

Children:
 437 F iv Gertrude GROSVENOR, b. 19 Feb 1867, Bartlett, OH.
 438 F v Theora Belle GROSVENOR, b. 17 Jan 1869, Bartlett,
    OH; d. 18 Jun 1931, Benton Harbor, MI. She m.
    Edwin Kendrick DYAR 28 Feb 1893, OH. Edwin, son of
    Joseph DYAR and Frances KENDRICK, b. 11 Feb 1866,
    Rainbow, OH; d. 4 Apr 1917.
 439 F vi Mary Henrietta GROSVENOR, b. 4 Apr 1872, Marietta,
    OH; d. 17 Aug 1919, CA.
    She m. William Alpha COOPER 17 Jun 1897.

259 Charles Henry GROSVENOR, b. 20 Sep 1833, Pomfret, CT; d. 30
Oct 1917, Athens, OH; bur. Union St. Cem., Athens, OH.
  Charles Henry GROSVENOR was educated in a log schoolhouse
at Athens County, Ohio. He taught school and studied law and
was admitted to the bar in 1857. In the Civil War he enlisted
in the 18th Ohio Regiment. He rose rapidly to Major and
became Brevet Brigadier General and commanded a regiment at
Chickamauga and at Missionary Ridge. At Marleville he
commanded a Brigade. He was mustered out on October 9, 1865.
  He was a presidential elector and a member of the Ohio
Legislature in 1872. He served as Speaker 1876-78. He was a
member of Congress in 1873 and from 1885-90 and 1892-1907. He
was a member of the Board of Trustees of the Ohio Soldiers and
Sailors Home in Xenia for eight years and President of the
Board for five years.
  He was a strongly partisan Republican and one of the
three leading debaters in the house of Representatives. He
and Champ Clark engaged in debates in front of Chautauqua
audiences. He was a delegate to the Republican Conventions of
1896 and 1902 and the author of a book on William McKinley and
a book of biographical sketches of the Presidents. He was
appointed Chairman of the Chickamauga and Chattanooga National
Park Commission in 1910 and served until his death in 1917.
(Congressional Biographies)
  Charles Henry GROSVENOR m. (1) Samantha STEWART 1 Dec
1850. Samantha, dau. of Daniel STEWART and Sarah CARTER, b.
5 Apr 1840, Stewarts Mills, OH; d. 2 Apr 1866, Athens, OH.

Children:
 440 F i Casette GROSVENOR, b. Aug 1863, Athens, OH; d. 27
    Jun 1864, Stewarts Mills, OH.
 441 F ii Constance Stewart GROSVENOR, b. 21 Dec. 1865,
    Athens, OH.
    She m. William Hollister MCKEE 27 Dec 1893.
    William, son of James MCKEE and Susan ARCHER, b. 8
    May 1865, Calais, OH.

SIXTH GENERATION

Charles m. (2) Louise Harriet CURRIER 21 May 1867. Louise, dau. of Jacob CURRIER and Harriet STEWART, b. 6 Dec 1843, Athens, OH.

Children:
        442 F iii Louise GROSVENOR, b. 23 Mar 1868, Athens, OH.
                   She m. Phelps Chapman LEETE 26 Jun 1894. Phelps, son of Horace LEETE and Ellen WETHERBEE, b. 19 Nov 1864, Andover, NY.
        443 M iv   Edward Lawrence GROSVENOR, b. 22 Oct 1869, Athens, OH; d. 21 Jul 1870.
        444 F v   Grace GROSVENOR, b. 16 Aug 1871, Athens, OH. She m. Cassius M. SHEPARD, MD 27 Nov 1900. Cassius, son of William SHEPARD and Georgeanna PATTICORD, b. 6 Mar 1872, Union, Morgan Co., OH.
        445 F vi   Helen GROSVENOR, b. 1 Nov 1875, Athens, OH; d. 5 Jul 1876, Oakland, MD.

261 Daniel Allan GROSVENOR, b. 4 Mar 1839, Rome, Ashtabula Co., OH; d. 16 Oct 1925.
        Daniel served for 3 years in the 3rd Regiment of the Ohio Volunteer Infantry in the Civil War.
        He was wounded at Perryvile, Kentucky and taken prisoner. He rejoined the army, was captured on a raid in Georgia and was imprisoned at Richmond. He was exchanged, and rejoined his regiment. (Bowen)
        Daniel Allan GROSVENOR m. Virginia LAMBORN 28 Oct 1874. Virginia, dau. of John LAMBORN and Matilda MORROW, b. 22 Apr 1851, Steubenville, OH.

Children:
+   446 M i   Frederick Lamborn GROSVENOR.
        447 F ii   Edith Louise GROSVENOR.
                   George Washington U., B.A. 1925, M.A. 1926. (Bowen)

271 Francis Dwight GROSVENOR, b. 22 Feb 1799, Sturbridge, MA.
        He m. (1) Julia COON 18 Dec 1823. Julia, b. 1795, Utica, NY; d. 16 Mar 1846.

Children:
+   448 M i   Charles Plimpton GROSVENOR.
        449 F ii   Harriet Haswell GROSVENOR, b. 1826.
        450 M iii John GROSVENOR, b. 1827, Utica, NY; d. CA.
        451 M iv   Chauncey Ward GROSVENOR, b. 1830.
+   452 M v   Graham Bethune GROSVENOR.
        453 M vi   George GROSVENOR.
+   454 M vii Thomas Walter GROSVENOR.
+   455M viii Edward Payson GROSVENOR.
        456 M ix   Oliver GROSVENOR, b. 1841.

Francis m. (2) Mary J. ALLYN 22 Feb 1847. Mary, dau. of Henry ALLYN and Asenath SCOVILLE, b. 5 Jun 1817, Coventry, Chenango Co., NY; d. 16 Oct 1869.

Child:
        457 F x   Julia Frances GROSVENOR, b. 1858.

273 Rev. Charles Payson GROSVENOR, b. 12 Aug 1804, Pomfret, Windham Co., CT; d. 23 Dec 1893, Palmer, MA.
        He m. (1) Hannah Hagadorn WELLS 8 Apr 1838. Hannah, dau. of Thomas WELLS and Maria POTTER, b. 8 May 1813, Kingston, RI; d. 6 Nov 1840.

Children:
        458 M i   Payson GROSVENOR, b. 3 Apr 1839, N. Scituate, MA; d. 28 Apr 1841, Pomfret, Windham Co., CT.
        459 F ii   Hannah Hagadorn GROSVENOR, b. 28 Oct 1840; d. 16 Feb 1904, Providence, RI.

        Rev. Charles m. (2) Elizabeth Eunice HARRISON 19 May 1842. Elizabeth, b. 11 Oct 1810, New Haven, CT; d. 4 Nov 1889.

Children:
        460 M iii Frederick Harrison GROSVENOR, b. 22 Jan 1848, Pomfret, Windham Co., CT; d. 28 May 1859, Pomfret, Windham Co., CT.
        461 M iv   Charles Francis GROSVENOR b. 10 Aug 1850, Rehoboth, MA. He m. (1) Lydia Mercelia ROYCE 10 Nov 1875. Lydia, dau. of Nelson ROYCE and Lydia GATES, b. 3 Sep 1848, Norwich, CT; d. 16 Sep 1900, Palmer, MA. He m. (2) Fanny W. BROWN 18 Mar 1902.

280 Oliver D. GROSVENOR, b. 2 Aug 1819; d. 1 Apr 1906.
        He m. Lewanthia R. (_____). Lewanthia, b. 2 May 1827; d. 4 Oct 1885.

Child:
        462 M i Oliver G. GROSVENOR, b. 13 Jan 1855; d. 17 Nov 1915.

294 David Augustus GROSVENOR, b. 31 Jan 1811, Manchester, MA; d. 27 Sep 1889, Danvers, MA.
        He m. Elizabeth Amelia FLINT 8 Jun 1837, Rutland, MA. Elizabeth, dau. of George FLINT and Joanna SYLVESTER, b. 26 Dec 1815.

Child:
+   463 M i   Milton John GROSVENOR, MD.

296 Edwin Prescott GROSVENOR, MD, b. 7 Sep 1820, Manchester, MA; d. 13 Dec 1856.
        He m. Harriet Ward SANBORNE. Harriet, dau. of Thayer SANBORN and Deborah WARD.

SIXTH GENERATION

Child:
+   464 M i   Edwin Augustus GROSVENOR.

297 Joseph Williston GROSVENOR, b. 1 May 1805, Paxton, MA; d. 19
     Apr 1838, Brookfield, MA.
          He m. Mary Bacon HANCOCK 7 May 1835, Barre, MA. Mary,
     dau of Nathaniel HANCOCK and Catherine LEE, b. 11 Feb 1817,
     Barre, MA.

Children:
     465 M i   Francis L. GROSVENOR, b. 17 Mar 1836, Petersham,
                MA.
     466 M ii   Joseph Williston GROSVENOR, b. 25 Jul 1837,
                Brookfield, MA; d. 19 Dec 1929.

300 David Rufus GROSVENOR, b. 25 Apr 1806, Paxton, MA; d. 11 Jul
     1889, Worcester, MA.
          He m. Irene Galland GODDARD 18 Mar 1829. Irene, dau. of
     Stephen GODDARD and Rachel WOODWARD, b. 27 Aug 1808; d. 23 Oct
     1849.

Children:
     467 M i   Lemuel Dwight GROSVENOR, b. 16 Feb 1830, Paxton,
                MA; d. 8 Sep 1914.
                He m. Elizabeth S. HINDS 17 Jan 1856, Petersham,
                MA. Elizabeth, dau. of Joseph HINDS and Susanna
                HEMENWAY, b. 1836, Petersham, MA.
     468 M ii   George Sumner GROSVENOR, b. 25 Nov 1831, Petersham,
                MA; d. 20 Mar 1931, Nice, FRA.
                He m. (1) Elizabeth Elvira PARMENTER 26 Dec 1859.
                Elizabeth, dau. of Joseph G. PARMENTER and Elvira
                CLAPP, b. 25 Jul 1833, Petersham, MA; d. 1 Sep
                1877.
                He m. (2) Cora McCoy BUNNELL 18 Jul 1878. Cora,
                dau. of Thomas BUNNELL and (_____) HORRIS, b. 2 Apr
                1836, Bridgeport, CT; d. 28 Oct 1926.
     469 M iii Rufus Henry GROSVENOR, b. 27 Aug 1835, Petersham,
                MA; d. 3 Oct 1886, Petersham, Ma.
                Rufus died a widower with two children. (Bowen)
     470 F iv   Ellen Lavina GROSVENOR, b. 16 Sep 1837, Petersham,
                MA; d. 2 Apr 1931, Petersham, MA.
                She m. John WILDER 27 Jan 1864, Petersham, MA.
                John, son of Nathaniel WILDER and Betsey MARCH, b.
                1832, Barre, MA.
     471 F v   Maria Frances GROSVENOR, b. 19 Nov 1839, Petersham,
                MA; d. 3 Nov 1877.
     472 F vi   Eliza Bigelow GROSVENOR, b. 29 Nov 1843, Petersham,
                MA; d. 8 Mar 1917.

301 Silas Newton GROSVENOR, b. 18 May 1808, Petersham, MA. He m.
     Mary CONANT.

Children:
    473 M i   Lemuel Conant GROSVENOR, MD, b. 22 Mar 1833, Paxton, MA; d. 15 Jul 1914, Taunton, MA.

                Lemuel was headmaster for seven years at the Mather School, Dorchester. He received his MD degree at Hance Medical College, Cleveland Ohio in 1864. He practiced medicine at Galesburg, IL and lectured on anatomy at Hahnemann Medical College, 1871-2. He was a professor at Chicago Homeopathic College from 1873 to 1899. He taught obstetrics at the Lincoln Park Training School for Nurses and authored the book "Our Babies." (Who's Who)

                Lemuel Conant GROSVENOR, MD m. (1) Ellen M. PROUTY 27 Feb 1865. Ellen d. 1874. He m. (2) Josephine BASSER 25 Jun 1877.

304 Jonathan Prescott GROSVENOR, b. 4 Aug 1816, Petersham, MA. He m. (1) Lydia E. FARRAR 8 Jun 1842.

Child:
    474 F i   Lydia S. GROSVENOR, b. 17 Nov 1845.

Jonathan m. (2) Rhoda Louise GODDARD 2 May 1849. Rhoda, dau. of Stephen GODDARD and Rachel WOODWARD, b. 1 Mar 1816, Petersham, MA.

306 Daniel Prescott GROSVENOR, b. 23 Jan 1805, Paxton, MA; d. 5 Oct 1882, Peabody, MA.
        He m. (1) Harriet PIERCE 23 Aug 1830, Paxton, MA. Harriet, dau. of Job PIERCE and Martha (___), d. Aug 1840, Paxton, MA.

Child:
+   475 M i   Daniel Prescott GROSVENOR.

Daniel m. (2) Lois KNIGHT 30 Dec 1843, Salem, MA. Lois, b. 14 Jul 1801, Salem, MA; d. 23 Nov 1886, Peabody, MA.

313 Samuel Avery GROSVENOR, b. 4 Dec 1815, Paxton, MA; d. 19 Oct 1850.
        He m. (1) Lois Rockwood PARTRIDGE 17 Oct 1844. Lois, dau. of Eleazar PARTRIDGE Jr. and Hannah KEITH, b. 1814; d. 24 Sep 1845, Paxton, MA.

Child:
    476 F i   Lois Partridge GROSVENOR, b. 19 Sep 1845, Paxton, MA.

Samuel m. (2) Marianne WATSON 16 Dec 1847. Marianne, dau. of Samuel WATSON and Sukey VICKERY, b. 1 May 1815, Leicester, MA; d. 6 Jul 1878.

333 Edward Nathan GROSVENOR, b. 16 Apr 1830, Mansfield, CT; d. 12 Dec 1917, Solon, MI; bur. Solon, MI.

Edward and his brother John operated a Scale Board Factory and a portable saw mill. The factory produced thin boards for picture backing and cheese boxes. Edward moved to Cedar Springs, Michigan, where he was listed on the Census of 1870 as the head sawyer in a mill. He joined the Masons and became Master of the lodge. He was a Justice of the Peace in 1875 and Township Clerk in 1876-7. The census of 1880 lists him as a Saw Mill Proprietor. (Jeanette Grosvenor)

Edward Nathan GROSVENOR m. (1) Susan CHAPPELL 22 Apr 1849. Susan, dau. of Benjamin CHAPPELL and Susan MOREY, b. abt 1827; d. 13 Nov 1881.

Children:
+   477 M i   Edward Austen GROSVENOR.
+   478 M ii George Orrin GROSVENOR.

Edward m. (2) Alzada WARRINER 20 Oct 1886. Alzada, d. 7 Dec 1904.

334 John Flavell GROSVENOR, b. 15 Jun 1832, Mansfield, CT; d. 20 Nov 1904, Claridon, OH.

John was a carpenter and a mill partner of Edward. (Jeanette Grosvenor)

John Flavell GROSVENOR m. Phebe NEWELL 10 Jul 1858. Phebe, dau of Harmon NEWELL and Loanna ENSIGN, b. 6 Jan 1834, Claridon, OH; d. 9 May 1912, Cleveland, OH.

Children:
     479 F i   Loanna GROSVENOR, b. 18 Jul 1867, Claridon, Geauga Co., OH; d. 21 Jan 1949, Cleveland, Cuyahoga Co., OH. She m. Henry MORGRET 3 Jun 1891, Claridon, OH. Henry, son of James MORGRET and Elizabeth (____), b. 22 Sep 1866, Hartville, Stark, OH; d. 9 Jun 1948.
               Children: Esther, Mary and Lectrus.
+   480 M ii Lectrus Newell GROSVENOR.

340 Col. William Mason GROSVENOR, b. 24 Apr 1835, Ashfield, MA; d. 20 Jul 1900, Englewood, NJ.

He m. Ellen Sage MARTIN 19 May 1859.

Children:
     481 F i   Kate GROSVENOR, b. 24 Dec 1859, New Haven, CT; d. 5 Aug 1889, Englewood, NJ.
               She m. Eldridge Merrick FOWLER 15 Dec 1887. Eldridge, son of Melzar FOWLER and Clarissa SPICER, b. 19 Aug 1833, Brownsville, NY; d. 7 Nov 1904, Pasadena, CA.
               Child: Kate Grosvenor Fowler

        482 F ii   Willa GROSVENOR, b. 1 Feb 1871, St. Louis, MO; d.
                   19 Mar 1872, St. Louis, MO.
+   483 M iii William Mason GROSVENOR.
        484 M iv   Richard GROSVENOR, b. Jul 1879, St. Louis, MO; d.
                   Jul 1879, St. Louis, MO.
        485 M v   Donald GROSVENOR, b. 1 Aug 1881, Englewood, NJ; d.,
                   Englewood, NJ.

345 Gordon GROSVENOR, b. 14 Aug 1789, Suffield, CT; d. 16 May
     1831. He m. (1) Laura PHELPS 1 Dec 1819, Suffield, CT.
     Laura, dau of Capt Seth PHELPS and Phoebe HASTINGS, b. 10 Dec
     1796; d. 25 Feb 1829

Children:
        486 F i   Mary Ann GROSVENOR, b. 16 Nov 1820, Suffield, CT.
                   She m. Leicester LEWIS 28 Sep 1841, Suffield, CT.
                   Leicester, son of James LEWIS and Desire REMINGTON,
                   b. 14 Oct 1817, Suffield, CT.
        487 M ii   Henry Phelps GROSVENOR, b. 11 Jan 1825, Suffield,
                   CT. He m. Mary KENT 22 Oct 1846. Mary, b. 1822;
                   d. 17 Aug 1858.
        488 F iii Margaret Lucy GROSVENOR, b. 15 Apr 1827; d. 24 Feb
                   1870. She m. Amos VANDERWERKEN. Amos, son of
                   Peter VANDERWERKEN and Sally GRIFFEN, b. 1826.
                   Children: Ellen, Charles, Eldora, and Lillian.

     Gordon GROSVENOR m. (2) Maria PHELPS 1 Dec 1829. Maria, b. 2
     Jan 1804, Suffield, CT; d. 17 Sep 1854, Lawrence, KS.

Children:
        489 F iv   Sarah GROSVENOR, b. 8 Dec 1831, Sharon, NY; d. 25
                   Jan 1853, Grosvenor Corners, NY.
+   490 M v   Judson GROSVENOR.

359 Chauncey GROSVENOR, b. 7 Sep 1799, Carlisle, NY; d. 27 Nov
     1880, Grosvenor Corners, NY.
         He m. Margaret BURHANS. Margaret, dau. of Barent BURHANS
     and Margaretha EIGNAAR, b. 3 Jul 1797, Oak Hill, NY; d. 9 May
     1879, Grosvenor Corners, NY.

Children:
+   491 M i   Amasa GROSVENOR.
        492 M ii   Charles GROSVENOR, b. 25 May 1825, Grosvenor
                   Corners, NY; d. 1915, Sloansville, NY.
        493 F iii Lucy GROSVENOR, b. 15 Apr 1827, Grosvenor Corners,
                   NY. She m. Amos VANDERWERKEN.
        494 F iv   Sarah GROSVENOR, b. 7 Dec 1831, Grosvenor Corners,
                   NY; d. 1849.
        495 M v   Judson GROSVENOR, b. 11 Oct 1837, Grosvenor
                   Corners, NY; d. 1913, Central Bridge, NY.
                   He m. Mary EKERSON.

360   George GROSVENOR, b. 27 Dec 1801, Carlisle, NY; d. 15 Mar
      1872, Grosvenor Corners, NY.
          He m. Catherine BEST 11 Feb 1821. Catherine, dau. of
      Henry BEST and Gertrude MINCKLER, d. 1888.

Children:
      496 M i   Charles GROSVENOR, b. 22 Dec 1821, Lawyersville,
                 NY; d. 1859.
  +   497 M ii   George Henry GROSVENOR.
      498 M iii Levi GROSVENOR, b. 12 Oct 1828; d. 1891.
                 He m. Louisa BOND.
      499 F iv   Emily GROSVENOR, b. 1829; d. 1913, Grosvenor
                 Corners, NY. She m. Peter FREDERICK. Peter, b.
                 1831; d. 1872, Grosvenor Corners, NY.
                 Children: Mary, Carrie Ella, Anna, and George.
  +   500 M v   Niram W. GROSVENOR.
  +   501 M vi   William Newton GROSVENOR.
  +   502 M vii Nelson Sidney GROSVENOR.
      503M viii Percy GROSVENOR, b. 1838; d. 1914
                 Listed in 1870 Census but not mentioned in father's
                 Will about 1870. (Bailey)
      504 M ix   Spenser GROSVENOR, b. 1838; d. 1910.
                 Listed in 1870 Census but not mentioned in father's
                 Will about 1870. (Bailey)

361   Niram GROSVENOR, b. 4 Mar 1804, Carlisle, NY; d. 19 Mar 1888,
      Grosvenor Corners, NY.
          He m. (1) Hannah UNDERHILL 11 Jun 1833. Hannah, dau. of
      Joel UNDERHILL and Phebe (_____), b. 19 Mar 1802; d. 12 Aug
      1848, Carlisle, NY.

Children:
      505 M i   Judson GROSVENOR, b. 15 Apr 1834; d. 1 Oct 1834.
      506 F ii   Sarah Jane GROSVENOR, b. 15 Oct 1835, Grosvenor
                 Corners, NY; d. 17 Mar 1906, Sloansville, NY.
                 She m. Newell GUFFIN. Newell, b. 16 Oct 1833; d.
                 27 Sep 1916.
                 Children: Romeyn, Lovillo, and Alfredo.
      507 M iii Percy GROSVENOR, b. 20 Jun 1837; d. 24 Mar 1838.
      508 F iv   Elizabeth Ellen GROSVENOR, b. 9 Mar 1839; d. 13 Jun
                 1923.
                 She m. (1) Samuel YOUNG 3 Oct 1859. Samuel, b. 3
                 Mar 1835; d. 11 Jun 1898, Grosvenor Corners, NY.
                 She m. (2) William YOUNG. William, b. 1841; d.
                 1922.

Niram m. (2) Martha Reese HAIGHT 7 Apr 1849, Carlisle, NY.
Martha, dau. of Martin REESE and Hanah RULIFSON, b. 27 Feb
1827, Millpoint, Montgomery Co., NY; d. 25 Jan 1912, Grosvenor
Corners, NY.

Children:
```
     509 F v    Augusta E. GROSVENOR, b. 3 Jan 1850, Grosvenor
                Corners, NY; d. 1 Apr 1938.
                She m. Milton HOLMES 3 Oct 1871. Milton, son of
                Judah HOLMES and Eliza DAVIS, b. 15 Nov 1850; d. 10
                May 1924.
                Children: Lovillo, Alfredo, Eva and Marjorie.
     510 F vi   Mary GROSVENOR, b. 8 Jan 1851, Grosvenor Corners,
                NY; d. 9 Feb 1852.
     511 F vii  Mary Frances GROSVENOR, b. 27 May 1852, Grosvenor
                Corners, NY; d. 5 May 1938
                She m. Anson CALKINS 13 Dec 1873. Anson, son of
                Alex CALKINS and Lucy LORD, b. 2 Jul 1853; d. 16
                Sep 1918.
                Children: Elbert, Edna, Samuel, Willis, Lealand,
                Lucy and Grover.
     512F viii  Emma Jane GROSVENOR, b. 9 Sep 1853, Grosvenor
                Corners, NY; d. 11 Mar 1854
+    513 M ix   Edgar Sharpe GROSVENOR.
+    514 M x    Henry Ward GROSVENOR.
+    515 M xi   Charles Wade GROSVENOR.
     516 F xii  Jennie Mae GROSVENOR, b. 6 Jun 1861, Grosvenor
                Corners, NY; d. 19 Mar 1864.
     517F xiii  Evaline May GROSVENOR, b. 18 Apr 1863, Grosvenor
                Corners, NY; d. 1 Jun 1882.
     518 M xiv  Willis Lee GROSVENOR, b. 15 Mar 1865, Grosvenor
                Corners, NY; d. 6 Mar 1909
+    519 M xv   Waldo J. GROSVENOR.
     520 F xvi  Ina Beulah GROSVENOR, b. 12 Dec 1869, Grosvenor
                Corners, NY; d. 15 May 1964.
                She m. Harry BAILEY 1 Sep 1897, Grosvenor Corners,
                NY. Harry, son of George BAILEY and Louise ERNST,
                b. 18 Mar 1872; d. 17 Jan 1956.
                Children: Kenneth, Lindsley and Robert.
```

```
364  Calvin GROSVENOR, b. 16 Sep 1810, Grosvnor Corners, NY; d. 20
     Mar 1890, Carlisle, NY.
         He m. Lavina YOUNG 7 Aug 1831. Lavina, dau. of John
     YOUNG and Dinah (____), b. abt 1811.
```

Child:
```
     521 M i    Charles GROSVENOR, b. 1831; d. 31 Jul 1839.
```

```
367  Rev. Parley GROSVENOR, b. 14 May 1820, Grosvenor Corners,
     Schoharie Co., NY; d. 11 May 1910, Chicago, IL.
         Rev. Parley m. (1) Mary UNDERHILL 1839. Mary, dau. of
     Joel UNDERHILL, b. 2 Jul 1819, Grosvenor Corners, Schoharie
     Co., NY; d. May 1847, Saratoga Springs, NY.
```

Child:
```
+    522 M i    Girdeon GROSVENOR.
```

Rev. Parley m. (2) Margaret GARDNER 18 Nov 1848, Carlisle, NY. Margaret, dau of Jonathan E. GARDNER and Corinthia BAUMIS, b. 7 May 1830, Grosvenor Corners, Schoharie Co., NY; d. 24 Apr 1899, Logan, IA.

Children:
```
      523 M.  ii  John Wellington GROSVENOR, b. 1850; d. 1884.
  +   524 M  iii  Calvin GROSVENOR.
  +   525 M   iv  Alvin Sharp GROSVENOR.
  +   526 M    v  Wardell GROSVENOR.
      527 F   vi  Mary GROSVENOR, b. 12 Dec 1858, Grosvenor Corners,
                  Schoharie Co., NY
                  She m. John Harold PUGH 15 Oct 1885.  John, son of
                  George PUGH and Elizabeth BARR, b. 15 Jan 1858,
                  Carrollton, OH.
                  Children:  Harold and Thomas.
      528 F  vii  Cora  GROSVENOR,  b.  1860,  Grosvenor  Corners,
                  Schoharie Co., NY.
  +   529M  viii  Douglas GROSVENOR.
      530 M   ix  Frank  GROSVENOR,  b.  5  Apr  1869,  Reeds  Cor.,
                  Livingston Co., NY.
                  He m. Lou PITTS 21 Dec 1904.  Lou, dau. of Stephen
                  PITTS and Mary SISSON, b. 26 Feb 1879, Woodbine,
                  IA.
```

371 Augustus Livingston GROSVENOR, b. 11 Mar 1808, Lebanon, Madison Co., NY; d. 29 Jan 1885.
He m. Cyrene Sophia GATES 17 Sep 1840, Lebanon, NY. Cyrene, dau. of Ezra GATES and Polly CAMPBELL, b. 2 Jun 1812; d. 3 Feb 1890.

Children:
```
      531 F    i  Olive Millicent GROSVENOR, b. 5 Mar 1842, Lebanon,
                  NY; d. 11 Jan 1915.
                  She m. John HARMON 30 Dec 1875.  John, son of
                  (_____) HARMON and Mary (_____), b. 5 Nov 1841, New
                  York, NY; d. 16 Feb 1926.
                  Chldren:  Mary and Martha.
  +   532 M   ii  George Griffin GROSVENOR.
```

372 Sydney Algernon GROSVENOR, b. 24 Oct 1809, Lebanon, Madison Co., NY; d. 27 Apr 1854.
Sydney m. Ellen Minerva WYLIE 9 Jul 1837. Ellen, dau. of Peter WYLIE and Lucretia HOLCOMB, b. 13 Aug 1813, Lebanon, Madison Co., NY; d. 16 Sep 1854.

Children:
```
      533 F    i  Margaret Elizabeth GROSVENOR, b. 17 Mar 1838,
                  Lebanon, NY; d. 15 Jun 1865.
      534 F   ii  Evelyn Minerva GROSVENOR, b. 23 Sep 1842, Lebanon,
                  NY; d. 8 Oct 1910, Hamilton, NY.
```

She m. James Eugene WEDGE 3 Jan 1867. James, son
of Marrit WEDGE and Mary STEDMAN, b. 17 Jan 1844,
Lebanon, NY; d. 31 Jul 1891, Hamilton, NY.

535 F iii Ellen Amelia GROSVENOR, b. 7 Dec 1845, Lebanon, NY;
d. 29 Dec 1915, Syracuse, NY.
She M. James Mott THROOP, MD 3 Mar 1870. James son
of William THROOP and California DUNBAR, b. 4 Jul
1838, Hubbardsville, NY; d. 15 May 1889.
Child: Henry.

536 M iv Eugene Franklin GROSVENOR, b. 29 Apr 1848, Lebanon,
NY; d. 16 Aug 1921.
He m. Mary Elizabeth DARROW 18 Jun 1873. Mary,
dau. of David DARROW and Mary ENOS, b. 1852, West
Eaton, NY; d. 22 Jun 1919.

379 Charles Williams GROSVENOR, b. 1 May 1839, Pomfret, Windham
Co., CT; d. 18 Jan 1922, Cambridge, MA.
He m. Elizabeth MATHEWSON 7 Mar 1866. Elizabeth, dau. of
George MATHEWSON and Hannah PAYSON, b. 28 Jul 1840, Pomfret,
Windham Co., CT; d. 22 Apr 1932, Cambridge, MA.

Children:
537 F i Mary Mathewson GROSVENOR, b. 4 Jan 1868, Pomfret,
Windham Co., CT; d. 24 Feb 1904.

538 F ii Julia Elizabeth GROSVENOR, b. 3 Feb 1871, Pomfret,
Windham Co., CT.
She m. George Amos PROCTOR 21 Feb 1912. George,
son of Amos PROCTOR and Margaret LIVINGSTON, b. 9
Jul 1852, Temple, NH.

539 M iii George Payson GROSVENOR, b. 28 Jul 1872, Pomfret,
Windham Co., CT; d. 23 Sep 1873.

540 F iv Louise Payson GROSVENOR, b. 7 Jan 1879, Pomfret,
Windham Co., CT; d. 29 Sep 1924.
Louise studied art in Philadelphia and Boston and
became a painter of portraits, landscapes and
marine scenes. She died on board the steamship
President Wilson. (Bowen)
Louise Payson GROSVENOR m. Wilhelm VAN DER LAN 7
Mar 1916. Wilhelm, son of Wilhelm VAN DER LAN and
Fredericka VOLLMAR, b. 15 Jan 1888, The Hague, NL.

380 Benjamin Hutchins GROSVENOR, b. 21 Sep 1841, Pomfret, Windham
Co., CT; d. 7 Apr 1923.
He m. Anna MATHEWSON 23 Dec 1867. Anna, dau of George
MATHEWSON and Hannah PAYSON, b. 30 Aug 1842, Pomfret, Windham
Co., CT; d. 3 Feb 1927, Pomfret, Windham Co., CT.

Children:
541 F i Charlotte Mathewson GROSVENOR, b. 9 Apr 1872,
Pomfret, Windham Co., CT.
+ 542 M ii John Payson GROSVENOR.

385   Edward Hutchins GROSVENOR, b. 12 Feb 1844, Pomfret, Windham
       Co., CT; d. 25 Mar 1927, Norwich, CT.
          He m. Elizabeth Jane WATT 12 Nov 1868. Elizabeth, dau.
       of James WATT and Isabelle BREMER, b. 7 Jul 1851, Salisbury,
       MA.

Children:
       543 F i   Josie GROSVENOR, b. Aug 1869.
       544 M ii   Herbert Edward GROSVENOR, b. 4 Jun 1871, Pomfret,
                  Windham Co., CT; d. 19 Aug 1926, Pomfret, Windham
                  Co., CT.
       545 F iii Isabelle Watt GROSVENOR, b. 8 Jun 1877.
                  She m. Omer John MILOT 8 Apr 1918. Omer, son of
                  Leger MILOT and Marie CARTIER, b. 17 Sep 1877,
                  Three Rivers, Can.
+   546 M iv   Walter James GROSVENOR.
+   547 M v   Thomas Hutchins GROSVENOR.
       548 M vi   Harold Leroy GROSVENOR, b. 21 Mar 1888, Pomfret,
                  Windham Co., CT; d. 8 Aug 1888.
+   549 M vii Frank Alexander GROSVENOR.

393   William GROSVENOR, b. 4 Aug 1838, Providence, RI; d. 20 Jun
       1896, Providence, RI.
          William Grosvenor graduated from Brown U. in 1860 and
       became his father's assistant in the Masonville Cotton Mfg Co.
       Upon the death of his father he became treasurer and then
       president of the Grosvenor-Dale Co., the largest manufacturer
       of cotton goods in Connecticut. William attended St. Johns
       Episcopal Church. (Cyclopedia, Vol 31).
          William GROSVENOR m. Rose Diamond PHINNEY 4 Oct 1882,
       Newport, RI. Rose, dau. of Theodore W. PHINNEY and Rose
       DIAMOND, b. 30 Jul 1857, Bristol, RI; d. 23 Jun 1924, Newport,
       RI.

Children:
       550 F i   Alice Mason GROSVENOR, b. 6 Aug 1883, Providence,
                  RI. She m. Dudley DAVIS 31 Aug 1908, Newport, RI.
                  Dudley, b. 21 Dec 1883, New York, NY.
                  Children: Dudley, Rose, William and Fellowes.
       551 F ii   Caroline Rose GROSVENOR, b. 9 Feb 1885, Providence,
                  RI. She m. Gilbert Maurice CONGDON 29 Mar 1910.
                  Gilbert, son of John CONGDON and Caroline BUFFIN,
                  b. 7 Jun 1887, Providence RI.
                  Children: William, Gilbert, Johns Hopkins, Robert
                  and Theodore.
+   552 M iii William GROSVENOR.
       553 F iv   Rose Phinney GROSVENOR, b. 13 Oct 1888, Providence,
                  RI. She m. George Peabody GARDNER Jr. 27 Jan 1913.
                  George, son of George Peabody GARDNER and Esther
                  BURNETT, b. 28 Jan 1888, Boston, MA.
                  Children born at Brookline, MA: Katherine,
                  Isabella, George, John, Rose and Robert.

554 M v   Robert GROSVENOR, b. 9 Apr 1892, Providence, RI; d. 27 Oct 1918, New York, NY.

555 F vi   Anita Diadamia GROSVENOR, b. 11 Mar 1895, Providence, RI.

+   556 M vii Theodore Phinney GROSVENOR.

400   Samuel Howe GROSVENOR, b. 10 Oct 1824, Pomfret, Windham Co., CT; d. 22 May 1888, Middletown, CT
          In 1934 Samuel's five daughters were living unmarried. His son had died unmarried. (Bowen)
          Samuel Howe GROSVENOR m. (1) Ursula Wolcott NOYES 9 Mar 1848. Ursula, dau. of Joseph NOYES and Sarah GURLEY, b. 21 Feb 1829, Lyme, CT; d. 12 Jan 1860.

Children:
557 F i   Sarah Elizabeth GROSVENOR, b. 22 Feb 1849, Norwich, CT.

558 F ii   Ellen Gurley GROSVENOR, b. 3 Nov 1850, Norwich, CT; d. 21 Mar 1926, Brooklyn, MD.

559 F iii Harriet Ely GROSVENOR, b. 23 Dec 1858, Norwich, CT.

Samuel m. (2) Maria Stryker MERCER 20 May 1862. Maria, dau. of Archibald MERCER and Harriet WHEAT, b. 2 Jan 1827, New London, CT; d. 7 Dec 1917, New York, NY.

Children:
560 M iv   Rev. William Mercer GROSVENOR, b. 22 Jun 1863, New London, CT; d. 16 Dec 1926. New York, NY.
           Rev. Wm Mercer GROSVENOR (Williams 1885, Berkley Divinity School 1888 and N.Y.U. 1898) served at Trinity Church, Lenox, MA; at Grace Church and Church of the Incarnation, NY City and was Dean of the Cathedral of St. John the Divine, NYC. He was the trustee of several colleges and of the Cathedral in which he is buried. (Bowen)

561 F v   Gertrude Mercer GROSVENOR, b. 20 Oct 1865, Brooklyn, NY.

562 F vi   Maria Ursula GROSVENOR, b. 11 Aug 1867, Brooklyn, NY.

SEVENTH GENERATION

401   Albert Barber GROSVENOR, DDS, b. 1852, Troy, Miami Co., OH
          Dr. Albert Barber Grosvenor was a Dentist at Springfield, OH. (Bowen)
          Albert Barber GROSVENOR, DDS m. Ada BROWN.

Children:
563 M i   Earl GROSVENOR.

564 M ii   Albert GROSVENOR.

402   William Daniel GROSVENOR, b. 18 Jun 1856, Troy, OH; d. 5 Mar 1907. He m. Mary Jane MITCHELL 18 Oct 1883. Mary, dau of

SEVENTH GENERATION

David MITCHELL and Ann MCCANDLESS, b. 11 Mar 1860, Piqua, OH; d. 15 Jan 1918.

Children:
565 M i Oliver Baer GROSVENOR, b. 4 Sep 1884, Piqua, OH. He m. Ferna Mae MURPHY 23 Jun 1910. Ferna, dau. of George MURPHY and Serilda BERRYHILL, b. 25 Dec 1882, Fletcher, OH.
566 M ii Mitchell David GROSVENOR, b. 14 Apr 1886, Piqua, OH.
567 F iii Ruth Alice GROSVENOR, b. 13 Jan 1890, Piqua, OH. She m. Loren GEPHART 4 Oct 1916. Loren, son of Jacob GEPHART and Dora KINSEY, b. 10 May 1890, Shelby Co., OH.
568 F iv Mary Frances GROSVENOR, b. 18 Feb 1893, Piqua, OH. She m. Charles STEPHENS 21 Jun 1916. Charles, son of Benjamin STEPHENS and Anna UNZICKER, b. 16 Feb 1894, Somerville, OH.

403 Edward Thornton GROSVENOR, MD, b. 31 Aug 1858, Richmond, IN. He m. Clara BECKER 17 Jan 1893. Clara, dau. of Fred BECKER and Elizabeth FABER, b. 16 Feb 1863, Detroit, MI.

Child:
569 F i Lavinia GROSVENOR, b. 15 Aug 1893, Detroit, MI. She m. Ray Fairman LEHOTE 15 Sep 1915. Ray, son of Eugene LEHOTE and Elda FAIRMAN, b. 23 Dec 1887, Milford, IL.

404 Elmer Baer GROSVENOR, MD, b. 29 Mar 1861, Union City, IN.
Elmer Baer was an Occulist (Opthamalogist) in Union City, Indiana. He graduated from Michigan Medical School and attended New York U post graduate school. He also studied at the Royal Opthalmic Hospital in London. He was a Presbyterian. (Abbey Grosvenor)
Elmer Baer GROSVENOR, MD m. Abbey JOHNSTON 13 Sep 1888, Van Buren Co., MI. Abbey, dau. of Daniel Webster JOHNSTON and June BATES, b. 21 Sep 1865, Richmond, IN.
Abbey studied Literature, History, and Archeology in France and Italy. She was a newspaper correspondent and an asociate editor. She also authored several books. She was a member of the DAR, a Presbyterian and a Democrat. She wrote genealogies of the Bates and Grosvenor families which were deposited at the Grosvenor (now Erie County) Library. (Who's Who)

Children:
570 M i Julius Johnston GROSVENOR, MD, b. 27 Jul 1889, Union City, IN; d. 8 Jan 1933.
Julius was a Physician, a graduate of Indiana U. (1912) and a First Lt. in the Medical Corp in WW1. Residence: Richmond, IN. (Abbey Grosvenor)

Julius Johnston GROSVENOR, MD m. (1) Abbey URBAN 1 Jun 1926. Abbey, dau of William URBAN and Minnie ESLINGER, b. 29 Aug 1885, Beaver Falls, PA; d. 17 Mar 1931.

He m. (2) Nora THALLS 24 Apr 1932. Nora, dau. of William THALLS and Susanna HEINE, b. 15 Jul 1895, Hagerstown, IN.

+ 571 M ii Elmer Johnston GROSVENOR.
   572 M iii Kenneth GROSVENOR, b. 9 Sep 1893; d. 11 Mar 1897.
+ 573 M iv Ivan Johnston GROSVENOR.

416 Fred Browne GROSVENOR, MD, b. 7 Nov 1885, Troy, Miami Co., OH; d. 9 Oct 1940, Woods, WI; bur. 15 Oct 1940, Greenlawn Cem. Columbus, Franklin Co., OH.

Fred Browne Grosvenor, the writer's father, graduated from Troy High School in 1904. In high school he played flute for the Rooster Band, a group of four students, and wrote articles for the school newspaper. He also played quarterback on the football team despite having had rheumatic fever at about age 12. He entered Ohio State University where he received his BS degree in 1908 and his MS degree in 1909.

He entered Michigan U. where he received his MD degree in 1911. He took a year of post graduate work and then went to Columbus, Ohio, where he married Olive Swickard, his college sweetheart.

They began housekeeping in Cincinnati where Browne worked as a physician at the Bethel Social Settlement. In 1914 Browne joined the faculty of Ohio State University as an instructor in diagnosis and materia medica. He taught there until 1922 except for a year off for military service.

In April 1918 he volunteered as a Lieutenant in the Medical Corp and was sent to Base Hospital 48 at Meseus-Bulay, France. The hospital was under construction and as soon as it was finished a trainload of equipment was received. This equipment was hardly in place when a trainload of 1100 wounded arrived from the front. Other trainloads arrived from the battles of Chateau-Thierry and the Argonne Forest. At one time he worked 24 hours without a break and had some heart trouble. This trouble came back to plague him later in life.

While these battles were going on it was the duty of the Officer of the Day to assign the incoming wounded to different hospital wards. The badly wounded men, who groaned from their wounds, were sent to a separate building under the care of a Chaplain while the rest of the men received attention from the Doctors. The "groaners," if still alive, were cared for later. He never liked to be Officer of the Day when the train loads came in. At the end of the war he was promoted to Captain. He was sent home in April 1919 and resumed his teaching at the University.

In 1922 he took up private practice at Cuyahoga Falls, Ohio. His office contained the only X-Ray machine in town. He worked long hours and made night calls when necessary. He relaxed from his work by playing golf and swimming and taking

annual hunting and fishing trips. By 1938 his heart trouble
had returned and he entered a Veteran's Hospital. He spent
much of the next two years in hospitals and died at Woods,
Wisconsin. He had been a member of the Masons, Elks, and
Rotary Club in Cuyahoga Falls. (RBG)

Fred Browne GROSVENOR, MD m. Olive Evangeline SWICKARD 31
Jul 1912. Olive, dau. of William Ellsworth SWICKARD and Olive
Charlotte PARK, b. 9 Nov 1885, Dayton, Montgomery Co., OH; d.
11 Mar 1984, Bloomington, IN; bur. Greenlawn Cem, Columbus,
Franklin Co., OH.

Olive Evangeline SWICKARD, the writer's mother, moved to
Westerville, Ohio, as a small child. She attended grade
school there and took her first year of high school at
Otterbein College. Here she began the study of piano and
started her long-time hobby of writing poetry. She later
wrote poems for her children and grand children and loved to
recite them when her eyes could no longer read them.

After her year at Otterbein her mother took the family to
Columbus, Ohio, where Olive attended High School and Ohio
State University. Olive majored in English and after
graduation taught sewing at the Y.W.C.A.

She married Fred Browne Grosvenor in 1912 and lived for
two years at Cincinnati and for eight years in Columbus. They
moved to Cuyahoga Falls in 1922 where she concentrated on
bringing up her children and followed her hobbies of piano
playing and composing. She encouraged her children to play
musical instruments and once organized an orchestra of
neighborhood children that played in public several times.

Browne developed heart trouble in 1938 and by 1939 was in
a Veteran's Hospital to stay. Olive took the family to her
mother's home in Columbus and lived there until Ted, the
youngest, finished High School in January 1942. She and Ted
then moved to Newton Falls, Ohio, and both sons worked in the
Ravenna Arsenal making war munitions. After Richard married
in 1943 she left to live near a child who could use her baby
sitting serices. She also worked as a companion for elderly
women in New York City.

In 1960 her children inherited a house at Troy, Ohio,
from their Aunt Clifford and they made it her home for the
next six years. In 1966 they transferred her to Florence's
New York home where she lived until 1971. At that time she
entered a nursing home at Waterloo, Ontario. In 1974 she
transferred to a nursing home at Bloomington, Indiana where
she lived until her death at age 98. (RBG)

Children:
+   574 M i   Richard Browne GROSVENOR.
+   575 F ii   Florence Olive GROSVENOR.
+   576 F iii Jean Frances GROSVENOR.
+   577 M iv   Theodore Park GROSVENOR.

417 Walter Reed GROSVENOR, b. 9 Mar 1848, Troy, Miami Co., OH; d.
     1 Jul 1931, Piqua, OH.

He m. Julia Ann MYERS 13 Jun 1872. Julia, dau. of John MYERS and Elizabeth ALE, b. 16 Feb 1850, Cincinnati, OH

Children:
+ 578 M i Charles George GROSVENOR.
  579 M ii Roy Watson GROSVENOR, b. 29 Sep 1874, Piqua OH; d. 16 Jul 1880.
  580 M iii Harry Clinton GROSVENOR, b. 26 Jun 1876, Piqua, OH; d. 18 Dec 1906.
  581 M iv Harley Edgar GROSVENOR, b. 25 Mar 1878, Piqua, OH; d. 4 Sep 1879.
+ 582 M v Earl Willis GROSVENOR.
  583 M vi Raymond L. GROSVENOR, b. 21 Sep 1881, Piqua, OH; d. 31 Oct 1906.
  584 M vii Frank Charles GROSVENOR, b. 16 Jun 1884, Piqua, OH.
+ 585M viii Vernon Myers GROSVENOR.

418 Napoleon P. GROSVENOR, b. abt 1826. He m. Sally Ann (____).

Child:
  586 F i Sophronia GROSVENOR, b. abt 1849.

432 John Harvey GROSVENOR, b. 13 Aug 1859, Canaan, Athens Co., OH. He m. Etta DODDS 25 Oct 1893. Etta, dau. of Clark DODDS and Harriet DEAN, b. 14 Dec 1848, Athens Co., OH; d. 19 Oct 1922.

Children:
  587 M i Charles Edgar GROSVENOR, b. 12 Dec 1894, Canaan, Athens Co., OH.
    He m. Luella COPELAND 5 May 1920. Luella, dau. of William COPELAND and Orra Inez OGG, b. 7 Dec 1900, Stewart, OH.
  588 M ii John Ernest GROSVENOR, b. 9 Feb 1899, Canaan, Athens Co., OH
    He m. Mary Imogene BOWMAN 20 Nov 1922. Mary, dau of Charles BOWMAN and Laura LINSCOTT, b. 21 Jun 1901, Rome, Ashtabula Co., OH.

446 Frederick Lamborn GROSVENOR, b. 8 Oct 1875, Athens, OH. He m. Clara May ECCARD 22 Feb 1899. Clara, dau. of Adolf ECCARD and Louisa SCHOENBORN, b. 22 Oct 1876, Washington, DC.

Children:
  589 F i Virginia Louise GROSVENOR, b. 27 Oct 1899, Washington, DC; d. 12 Dec 1915
  590 F ii Helen Augusta GROSVENOR, b. 29 Jun 1903, Washington, DC. She m. Abel HABERMAN 11 Feb 1923
  591 F iii Margaret Lamborn GROSVENOR, b. 17 Jun 1905, Washington, DC. She m. Joseph Albert BLANKEN 15 Dec 1926.
    Children: Richard and Raymond

592 F iv Edith Eccard GROSVENOR, b. 13 Jun 1913, Washington, DC.

448 Charles Plimpton GROSVENOR, b. 18 Oct 1824, Utica, NY; d. 7 Sep 1865. He m. Abbe LYON Dec 1848.

Children:
593 F i Julia Lyon GROSVENOR, b. 20 May 1850. She m. Franklin PHILLIPS 6 Jun 1893.
594 F ii Ida B. GROSVENOR, b. 18 Jun 1851. She m. Franklin WARREN 22 Feb 1881.
Children: Julia and Hannah.
595 F iii Kate GROSVENOR, b. 29 Mar 1853, Utica, NY. She m. William A. COMSTOCK 25 Nov 1874. William, son of William C. COMSTOCK and Sarah E. HODGES, b. 25 Jun 1845.
Child: William

452 Graham Bethune GROSVENOR, b. 13 Dec 1833; d. 18 Jan 1927.
Graham organized the Grosvenor Grays, the first company from Iowa to enter the Civil War. He was a teacher and instrumental in spreading literature and education among the early settlers. (Burke)
Graham Bethune GROSVENOR m. Martha Louise HARGER.

Children:
596 F i Anna Louise GROSVENOR, b. 6 Jun 1858, Dubuque, IA; d. 22 Oct 1925, Scarsdale, NY.
She m. George Nicholas FARWELL 18 Apr 1880. George, son of John FARWELL and Martha Ann COOPER, b. 3 Jan 1858, Claremont, NH; d. 31 Dec 1922, Scarsdale, NY.
+ 597 M ii George Benton GROSVENOR.

454 Thomas Walter GROSVENOR, b. 1835, Utica, NY; d. Chicago, IL.
He m. Mary GROSVENOR. Mary, dau. of Godfrey GROSVENOR.

Child:
598 M i Thomas Walter GROSVENOR Jr.

455 Edward Payson GROSVENOR, b. 1 Dec 1837, Utica, NY.
He m. Addie Louise HOWARD 19 Nov 1871. Addie, dau. of John HOWARD and Mary A. AYRES, b. 8 Jan 1848, Main Village, NY.
Children:
599 M i Thomas Howard GROSVENOR, b. 22 Jun 1874, Manhattan, IA; d. 11 Dec 1927.
He m. Bernice RICKMAN 27 Sep 1910. Bernice, dau. of Columbus RICKMAN and Isabel GERKING, b. Umatilla Co., OR.
600 F ii Genevieve Ward GROSVENOR, b. 14 Dec 1876, Dubuque, IA. She m. Charles E. OWENS, Charles, son of Evan OWENS and Eliza SIMMONS.

463 Milton John GROSVENOR, MD, b. 15 Apr 1839, Danvers, MA; d. 20
     Sep 1917, Middleton, MA.
          He m. Mary Irene PAUL 10 Dec 1862. Mary, dau. of John
     PAUL and Sarah (____), b. 12 Aug 1843, Lowell, MA.

Child:
     601 M i   John Milton GROSVENOR, b. 22 Apr 1864, Danvers, MA;
                d. 1928, Swampscott, MA

464 Edwin Augustus GROSVENOR, b. 30 Aug 1845, Newburyport, MA.
          Edwin Augustus GROSVENOR graduated from Amherst in 1867,
     and from Andover Theological Seminary in 1872. He was an
     educator and author. He taught history, government and
     international law at Robert's College, Constantinople, Turkey
     from 1873 to 1915 except for two years of teaching history at
     Smith College. He traveled widely in Europe and the East
     lecturing on historical and diplomatic subjects and became
     known to scholars and diplomats. He had an immense knowledge
     of oriental languages.
          He was author of "Constantinople," 2 volumes in 1895 that
     is a standard authority. He wrote numerous articles on
     European History and International Relations including 300
     articles in the Universal Cyclopedia. He was president of the
     United Chapters of Phi Beta Kappa. (Cyclopedia Vol. 10)
          Edwin Augustus GROSVENOR m. Lillian Hovey WATERS 23 Oct
     1873. Lillian, dau. of Col. Asa Holman WATERS and Mary
     Elizabeth HOVEY, b. 30 Aug 1845; d. 9 May 1931, Amherst, NJ.

Children:
+   602 M i   Gilbert Hovey GROSVENOR.
+   603 M ii   Edwin Prescott GROSVENOR.
+   604 M iii Asa Waters GROSVENOR.
     605 F iv   Harriet Sanborne GROSVENOR, b. 15 Apr 1890,
                Constantinople, Turkey; d. 1 Jun 1890.

475 Daniel Prescott GROSVENOR, b. 6 Sep 1836, Paxton, MA; d. 15
     Sep 1919, Winthrop, MA.
          He m. Mary Ann SMITH 11 Oct 1866. Mary, dau. of Samuel
     SMITH and Abigail FIFIELD, b. 7 May 1846, Woodstock, VT; d. 15
     Aug 1932.

Children:
     606 F i   Harriet Percy GROSVENOR, b. 31 Mar 1869, Peabody,
                MA; d. 23 Dec 1901.
                She m. Joseph Loomis DANA 14 Feb 1893. Joseph, son
                of Charles DANA and Charity LOOMIS, b. 6 Mar 1865,
                Woodstock, VT.
     607 F ii   Mary Agnes GROSVENOR, b. 25 Dec 1873, Peabody, MA.
                She m. Charles Browne PRICE 5 Jun 1895. Charles,
                son of Charles H. PRICE and Fannie PETTINGELL, b.
                22 Oct 1869, Salem, MA.
                Children: Virginia and Charles.

SEVENTH GENERATION

608 F iii Frances Fox GROSVENOR, b. 17 Sep 1880, Peabody, MA;
           d. Mar 1923.
609 F iv   Isabel Graves GROSVENOR, b. 17 Sep 1880, Peabody,
           MA; d. May 1881.
610 M v   Prescott GROSVENOR, b. Nov 1884, Peabody, MA; d.
           Jul 1899.

477 Edward Austen GROSVENOR, b. 23 Aug 1853, Mansfield, CT; d. 17
     Jul 1910, Edneyville, Henderson Co., NC.
          He m. Gezelle BEACH. Gezelle, dau. of Russell BEACH and
     Charlotte DUMON, b. 17 Nov 1852, Otisu, MI; d. 14 Jan 1945,
     Flint, MI.

Children:
     611 M i   Herbert Leroy GROSVENOR, b. 2 Aug 1880, MI; d. 24
                Feb 1955, Kansas City, MO.
                Herbert operated a store in Detroit and moved to
                Brooklyn where he worked on boats.
                Herbert Leroy GROSVENOR m. Bessie BROWN. Bessie,
                dau. of Irwin BROWN and Josephine STONE, b. 2 Apr
                1885; d. 7 Feb 1946.
 +   612 M ii   Leonard Arthur St. John GROSVENOR.
     613 F iii Daisy GROSVENOR, b. 12 Sep 1883, White Cloud, MI;
                d. 20 May 1935, Flint, MI.
                She m. (1) David BISSELL.
                She m. (2) Richard MORRILL.
     614 F iv   Nina GROSVENOR, b. 27 Aug 1886, Alma, MI; d. 1 Sep
                1936, Flint, MI.
                She m. William STRACHEY 1 Jul 1904.
                Children: Reginald and Ella.

478 George Orrin GROSVENOR, b. 6 Feb 1863, Claridon, OH; d. 12 Dec
     1930, Muskegon, MI.
          He m. Lowella RICHARD 3 Jul 1890, White Cloud, MI.
     Lowella, dau. of Augustus RICHARD and Olive (_____).

Children:
     615 F i   Belva Fern GROSVENOR, b. 25 Apr 1891, White Cloud,
                MI. She m. Harry JOHNSON 3 Jul 1913, Traverse
                City, MI. Harry, b. 12 Mar 1888, Gills Pier, MI; d.
                30 Mar 1963, Holton, MI.
                Children: Tresa, Kimberly, Terri and George.
 +   616 M ii   George Tracy GROSVENOR.
     617 F iii Iva GROSVENOR, b. 18 May 1892, Wile Twp., MI; d. 19
                Apr 1959, Muskeson, MI Iva had three marriages.

480 Lectrus Newell GROSVENOR, b. 7 Aug 1862, Claridon, Geauga Co.,
     OH; d. 6 May 1947, Chardon, Geauga Co., OH.
          Lectrus was a farmer and a produce dealer and owned a
     cider mill. He traveled with a crew to farms to harvest
     produce and peddled cider, produce and maple syrup on a
     regular route in Painsville and Fairport, OH. He was a member
     of the Claridon Congregational Church, the Knights of Pythias

and the Grange. At one time he served as Township Trustee.
(Jeanette Grosvenor)
     Lectrus Newell GROSVENOR m. Flora Belle HATHWAY 1891.
Flora, dau. of John HATHWAY and Adeline POTTER, b. 6 May 1869,
E. Claridon, OH; d. 11 Aug 1935, Chardon, OH.

Children:
     618 F i   Ruth GROSVENOR, b. 27 Jul 1892, Claridon, Geauga
           Co., OH; d. Claridon, Geauga Co., OH.
           Ruth m. Richard MOODY 5 May 1913, Windsor, OH.
           Richard, son of Myron MOODY and Mary FARZS, b. 8
           Dec 1884, Windsor, Ashtabula Co., OH; d. 14 May
           1948.
           Child: Theodore
+   619 M ii   Ralph Collins GROSVENOR.
     620 F iii Theodoris GROSVENOR, b. 25 Apr 1905, Claridon,
           Geauga Co., OH; d. 21 Sep 1969, Chardon, Geauga
           Co., OH
           She m. Edward Ames PARKS 10 Feb 1934, Linesville,
           Crawford, PA. Edward, b. 12 Aug 1907, Chardon,
           Geauga Co., OH
           Children: Mary Jane and Daniel.

483 William Mason GROSVENOR, b. 5 Oct 1873.
     William Mason earned his B.S. at Polytechnical Institute,
Brooklyn, 1893, and his Ph.D at the University of Pennsylvania
1898. He was a Chemical Engineer. He was a Consulting
Engineer at New York City and a member of the WW1 National
Defense Council. He held numerous U.S. Patents and was the
first to introduce high speed moving pictures and projection
to analyze motion of industrial work. (Who's Who) (Bowen)
     William Mason GROSVENOR m. Marie Celine DEXTER 9 Apr
1901, Detroit, MI. Marie, dau. of Stephen CHAMBERLAIN and
Celia COMSTOCK, b. 19 May 1868, Waverly, NY. Celia COMSTOCK
was divorced from Stephen CHAMBERLAIN and m. Jeremiah Newton
DEXTER about 1870. Marie Celine Chamberlain took her
stepfather's name.

Children:
     621 F i   Mary Dexter GROSVENOR, b. 18 Jul 1902, New York,
           NY. She m. Ralph Oliver ELLSWORTH 30 Apr 1929.
           Ralph, son of Charles ELLSWORTH and Bertha
           BRINKERHOFF, b. 2 Aug 1902.
     622 M ii   William Mason GROSVENOR, b. 2 Sep 1905, Buffalo,
           NY. William was educated at Antioch College,
           M.I.T., and Columbia U. (Burke) (Bowen)
           William Mason GROSVENOR m. Rose HOBART (legal
           professional name) 9 Oct 1932. Rose, dau. of Paul
           KEFER and Marguerite BUSS, b. 1 May 1906, New York,
           NY.

490 Judson GROSVENOR, b. 11 Oct 1837, Grosvenor Corners, NY; d.
     1913, Central Bridge, NY.

SEVENTH GENERATION

He m. Mary Ette UNDERHILL 11 Oct 1879. Mary, dau. of
Darius UNDERHILL and Clarissa CHICHESTER, b. 17 May 1845.

Child:
    623 F i   Bessie GROSVENOR, b. 1881, Grosvenor Corners, NY;
              d. 1896.

491 Amasa GROSVENOR, b. 23 Nov 1821, Grosvenor Corners, NY; d.
     1895. He m. Rachel GARDNER 8 May 1844. Rachel, dau. of
     Jonathan GARDNER and Corinthia MOSHER, b. 10 Jul 1826; d. 14
     Feb 1865.

Children:
    624 M i   Washington Irving GROSVENOR, b. 28 Apr 1845; d. 21
              Feb 1925, Cobleskill, NY.
              Washington was deacon of Sloansville Baptist Church
              and Supervisor at Esperance, NY. (Bowen)
    625 F ii Melissa GROSVENOR, b. 4 Jan 1847, Grosvenor
              Corners, NY.
              She m. Martin Luther BASSETT. Martin, son of
              Francis BASSETT and Polly RANDALL, b. 12 Sep 1837.
              Children: Rhobie, Edna, Mina and Floyd.
    626 F iii Amelia GROSVENOR, b. 15 Nov 1848, Grosvenor
              Corners, NY; d. 21 Jun 1849.
    627 F iv Lucy Marlin GROSVENOR, b. 13 Nov 1850, Grosvenor
              Corners, NY; d. 13 Feb 1926, Hickory, NC.
              She m. Leander FLAGLER. Leander, b. Grosvenor
              Corners, NY; d. Mar 1934, High Point, NC
              Children: Fred and Alice.
    628 F v   Sarah GROSVENOR, b. 18 Sep 1853, Grosvenor Corners,
              NY; d. bef 1895.
    629 F vi Alice GROSVENOR, b. 12 Jun 1856, Grosvenor Corners,
              NY; d. 1864.
    630 F vii Selena GROSVENOR, b. 14 May 1858, Grosvenor
              Corners, NY; d. 1896.
              She m. Henry D. GUFFIN 30 Jul 1879. Henry, son of
              Jonathan GUFFIN and Sarah TAYLOR, b. 14 Apr 1854;
              d. 1897.
    631F viii Ellen Madrilla GROSVENOR, b. 12 Jun 1863, Grosvenor
              Corners, NY; d. 27 Mar 1934, Oak Ridge, NY.
              She m. John HERRICK 23 Apr 1881. John, son of
              Elisha HERRICK and Susan EATON, b. 29 Dec 1853,
              Charleston, Montgomery Co., NY; d. 6 Jul 1928, Oak
              Ridge, NY.
              Children: Stanley, Ray, Lester and Mae.

497 George Henry GROSVENOR, b. 3 Oct 1826; d. 6 May 1891.
     He m. Mary YOUNG 4 Sep 1850, Schoharie Co., NY. Mary,
     dau. of Matthew YOUNG and Nancy MCMILLEN, b. 23 Oct 1827; d.
     9 Jun 1890, Grosvenor Corners, NY.

Children:

> 632 F i   Annette GROSVENOR, b. 3 Mar 1851; d. 23 Aug 1931. She m. Nelson S. YOUNG 25 Dec 1870. Nelson, b. 2 Apr 1850; d. 22 Apr 1917.
> Child: Clarence.

+   633 M ii   Millard GROSVENOR.

> 634 M iii Charles M. GROSVENOR, b. 29 Aug 1857; d. 6 Nov 1941. He m. Sarah GUFFIN 11 Oct 1883.

500 Niram W. GROSVENOR, b. 9 Oct 1832; d. 1911, Grosvenor Corners, NY. He m. Lavina YOUNG 11 Dec 1860, Carlisle, NY. Lavina, dau. of Joshua YOUNG and Magdalena BORST, b. 24 Mar 1837, Carlisle Center, NY; d. 1912, Grosvenor Corners, NY.

Children:

> 635 M i   Elmer GROSVENOR, b. 22 Mar 1862; d. 21 Mar 1864.
> 635 F ii   Atalee GROSVENOR, b. 29 Jan 1865. She m. (1) William ARNOLD Jul 1883.
> Child: Florence
> Atalee GROSVENOR m. (2) William B. FELTER 7 Mar 1894. William, b. 5 Jan 1867, Newburg, NY.
> 637 F iii Cora GROSVENOR, b. 1863.

501 William Newton GROSVENOR, b. 8 Oct 1834; d. 1912. He m. Eliza (_____); they divorced.

Child:

> 638 M i   William GROSVENOR Jr.

502 Nelson Sidney GROSVENOR, b. 9 Feb 1836; d. 14 Aug 1905. He m. Delana CRAMER 5 Oct 1859. Delana, dau. of Frederick CRAMER and Susan (_____), b. 4 Nov 1837; d. 29 Oct 1921; bur., Johnston, NY.

Children:

> 639 F i   Adelaide GROSVENOR, b. 8 Sep 1860; d. 7 Sep 1955. She m. Charles DINGMAN. Charles, son of Elijah DINGMAN and Elizabeth DEVINNE, b. 1848.
> Children: Stratton and Lula.
> 640 F ii   Nora GROSVENOR, b. 8 Jun 1862; d. 25 May 1959. She m. Jesse MCNEIL 29 Oct 1881, Carlisle, NY. Jesse, son of Alexander MCNEIL and Jane (_____), b. 13 Jun 1858, Carlisle, NY; d. 23 May 1937.
> Child: Lillian.

+   641 M iii Arthur GROSVENOR.

> 642 F iv   Lucy GROSVENOR, b. 1 Jan 1869; d. 9 Aug 1960. She m. Frederick E. BEEKMAN 4 Nov 1891. Frederick, b. 10 May 1863.
> Child: Freda.
> 643 F v   Isabelle GROSVENOR, b. 7 Sep 1871. She m. Arthur MILES. Arthur, b. 1892.
> Children: Jessie and Gifford.

+   644 M vi Sidney GROSVENOR.

645 F vii Allie GROSVENOR, b. 29 Oct 1876; d. 22 Nov 1943.
She m. Jay ELDRIDGE 9 Apr 1902. Jay, son of William ELDRIDGE and Lavinia (____).
Children: Esther and Frederick.
646M viii William GROSVENOR, b. abt 1879.

513 Edgar Sharpe GROSVENOR, b. 12 Feb 1855, Grosvenor Corners, NY: d. 16 Dec 1938. He m. (1) Adelaide MCCULLOCH 1 Sep 1876. Adelaide, dau. of John MCCULLOCH and Lucy BRODT, b. 24 Jul 1853; d. 16 Sep 1918.

Children:
647 F i Nellie Van GROSVENOR, b. 26 Apr 1877; d. 29 Nov 1967. She m. Rufus RICHTMYER 11 Mar 1897. Rufus, b. 1 Oct 1870; d. 22 Nov 1958.
648 M ii Roy McCulloch GROSVENOR, b. 9 May 1878; d. 29 Apr 1913.
649 M iii Virgil C. GROSVENOR, b. 30 Aug 1880; d. 20 Dec 1956. He m. Lena SAFFORD 1910. Lena, dau. of Ford SAFFORD and Martha GORDON, b. 17 Apr 1891.
650 F iv Una GROSVENOR, b. 7 Feb 1882; d. 3 Feb 1916. She m. Harry RICHTMYER. Harry, b. abt 1876. Children: Mildred and Wilma.
651 F v Eva GROSVENOR, b. 2 Feb 1883. She m. Earle B. DECKER Feb 1916.
652 F vi Claire GROSVENOR, b. 1884; d. 1891.
653 M vii John GROSVENOR, b. 1890; d. 1891.
654F viii Hazel GROSVENOR, b. 4 May 1892; d. 20 Apr 1902.

Edgar m. (2) Ellen ROCKEFELLER. Ellen d. 1928.

514 Henry Ward GROSVENOR, b. 23 Apr 1857, Grosvenor Corners, NY; d. 3 Jan 1943.
He m. Harriet Louise RELYEA 15 Aug 1878. Harriet, dau of John RELYEA and Delia BASSETT, b. 1 Mar 1861, Grosvenor Corners, NY; d. 6 Apr 1919.

Child:
+   655 M. Verner Calvin GROSVENOR.

515 Charles Wade GROSVENOR, b. 9 Mar 1859, Grosvenor Corners, NY; d. Nov 1941.
Charles m. Bertha TALMADGE, Bertha, dau. of Isaac TALMADGE and Melissa BARLOW, b. 20 Aug 1859; d. 15 Dec 1919.

Children:
656 M i Earle GROSVENOR, b. 9 Dec 1885; d. 19 Feb 1886.
657 F ii Ethel GROSVENOR.

519 Waldo J. GROSVENOR, b. 18 Oct 1867, Grosvenor Corners, NY; d. 9 Jul 1936.
He m. Annie F. O'BRYAN. Annie, dau. of Jacob O'BRYAN and Katherine KENNEDY, b. 28 Jun 1873; d. 2 Nov 1944.

SEVENTH GENERATION

Children:
+   658 M i   Ernest GROSVENOR.
      659 M ii   Ralph GROSVENOR, b. 5 Dec 1893.
                  He m. Ramona LIPSNER 29 Mar 1935, New York, NY.
                  Ramona, dau. of Maximalian LIPSNER and Sarah
                  (____), b. 5 Jul 1897.
      660 F iii   Martha Dorothy GROSVENOR, b. 27 Feb 1900; d. 3 Oct
                  1970. She m. (1) John WILLIAMS abt 1921; they
                  divorced.
                  She m. (2) Clarence DINGMAN 6 Sep 1941. Clarence,
                  b. 6 Feb 1903; d. 27 Jan 1972
+   661 M iv   Willis Lee GROSVENOR.

522   Girdeon GROSVENOR, b. 7 Feb 1840, Grosvenor Corners, Schoharie
      Co., NY; d. 21 Sep 1921.
          He m. Phebe BURNIGHT 25 Dec 1867. Phebe, dau. of Nathan
      BURNIGHT and Eliza FOX, b. 24 Feb 1847, Bowens Prairie, IA; d.
      9 Jun 1918.

Children:
      662 F i   Ellen GROSVENOR, b. 4 Sep 1871, Council Bluffs, IA.
                  She m. Charles PICKNEY 30 Nov 1893. Charles, son
                  of Alpheus PICKNEY and Julia CHAPMAN, b. 31 Mar
                  1870, Navarino, NY.
                  Children: Virginia, Julia, and Nathan.
      663 F ii   Caroline Selina GROSVENOR, b. 18 Jan 1876, Council
                  Bluffs, IA.
                  She m. Henry WAGECK 6 May 1901. Henry, son of Adam
                  WAGECK and Elizabeth SCHLUND, b. 19 Oct 1874,
                  McGregor, IA.
                  Children: Henry, Donald, and Mildred.
      664 F iii   Mary Frances GROSVENOR, b. 5 Feb 1878, Council
                  Bluffs, IA.
                  She m. Theodore THOLL 26 Aug 1903. Theodore, son
                  of Peter THOLL and Mary KIRSCH, b. 10 Apr 1879,
                  Council Bluffs, IA.
                  Children: Dorothy, Catherine, Jane and Pheobe.
      665 F iv   Almyra Louise GROSVENOR, b. 13 Jul 1880, Council
                  Bluffs, IA.
                  She m. Bert CAUGHEY 25 Jul 1901. Bert, son of Finn
                  CAUGHEY and Sara CLIFFORD, b. 30 Jan 1887, Council
                  Bluffs, IA.
                  Children: Arthur and unnamed child.
+   666 M v   Girdeon Parley GROSVENOR Jr.
      667 F vi   Sarah Millard GROSVENOR, b. 28 Feb 1885, Council
                  Bluffs, IA.
                  She m. Fred GREENE 23 Dec 1908. Fred, son of Fred
                  GREENE and Mary HUSSER, b. 25 Mar 1884.
                  Children: Virginia, Eugene, Ethel and Fred.
      668 F vii   Hattie GROSVENOR, b. Council Bluffs, IA.

524   Calvin GROSVENOR, b. 1 May 1852, Grosvenor Corners, Schoharie
      Co., NY; d. 21 Nov 1948.

He m. Clara MAGNUM 5 Jul 1881. Clara, dau. of Alcephas MAGNUM and Jane IRVIN, b. 24 Jun 1859, Van Buren Co., IA; d. 13 Nov 1933.

Children:

669	M	i	Floyd Magnum GROSVENOR, b. 27 Mar 1884, Logan, Harrison Co., IA; d. 31 May 1930.
670	M	ii	Otis Sharp GROSVENOR, b. 17 Dec 1885, Logan, Harrison Co., IA.
671	M	iii	Willard GROSVENOR, b. 20 Apr 1888, Council Bluffs, IA.
672	M	iv	Irvy Calvin GROSVENOR, b. 6 Nov 1890, Logan, Harrison Co., IA.

He m. Thelma COYLE 1 Feb 1922. Thelma, dau. of Nathaniel COYLE and Edith ELLISON, b. 23 Mar 1898, Woodbine, IA.

673	F	v	Alice Clara GROSVENOR, b. 27 Apr 1893, Logan, Harrison Co., IA.

She m. Harry PLATH 25 Dec 1916. Harry, son of Herman PLATH and Anna METHER, b. 7 Apr 1893, Logan, IA.
Children: Marjory, Virgil, Evelyn, Hubert and Phyllis.

674	F	vi	Ruth Kathryn GROSVENOR, b. 14 Aug 1896, Logan, Harrison Co., IA; d. 1974/1975.

She m. Ursin GOODMAN 14 Aug 1917. Ursin, son of John GOODMAN and Winnie HILDERBRANDE, b. 1893, Algansee, Brand Co., MI.
Children: Kathryn, John, Roberta, Patricia and Floyd.

525 Alvin Sharp GROSVENOR, b. 5 Jul 1854, Grosvenor Corners, Schoharie Co., NY; d. 7 Feb 1923.
        He m. Mary KILTS. Mary, b. abt 1856.
Children:

675	F	i	Edna GROSVENOR m. Lewis LARSON.
676	F	ii	Ada GROSVENOR. She m. (____) ETCHISON.
677	M	iii	Charles Lewis GROSVENOR.

526 Wardell GROSVENOR, b. 1856, Grosvenor Corners, NY. He m. Nellie JEFFERS.

Children:

+	678	M	i	Julius GROSVENOR.
	679	M	ii	Herman GROSVENOR.
	680	F	iii	Bessie GROSVENOR, b. Feb 1892. She m. Ray ROCKWELL.

Children: Lee, Marie, Homer, Doris, Alice, Charles, Mary Ellen, Virginia and Edith.

	681	M	iv	Horace Wardell GROSVENOR, b. 9 Sep 1894.

He m. Marie MICHAEL.

+	682	M	v	Homer Douglas GROSVENOR.
+	683	M	vi	Thomas GROSVENOR.

529   Douglas GROSVENOR, b. 1862, Grosvenor Corners, Schoharie Co.,
      NY; d. 1915. He m. Emma JEFFERS.

Children:
      684 F   i   Grace GROSVENOR m. Charles O'DELL.
                   Children: Bernadine and Doris.
      685 F   ii   Hazel GROSVENOR m. Cecil BOYLE.
      686 M   iii Fred GROSVENOR.
      687 F   iv   Florence GROSVENOR m. Joe PHLARATY.
                   Children: Phyliss, Charles, Miles and Agnes.
      688 F   v   Margaret GROSVENOR m. Charles POTTER.
      689 F   vi   Shirley GROSVENOR m. Charles CLARK.
      690 F   vii Clara GROSVENOR m. Charles BENNETT.
      691M viii   Bryon GROSVENOR m. June Payne.
      692 F   ix   Edna GROSVENOR.
      693 F   x   Vashti GROSVENOR.
      694 F   xi   Inez GROVENOR m. Edward KILBLOCK.
                   Child: Merna Lee.

532   George Griffin GROSVENOR, b. 27 Apr 1845, Lebanon, NY; d. 17
      Jan 1923.
           He m. Sara MAKIN 12 Nov 1872, West Eaton, NY. Sara, dau
      of Webster MAKIN and Caroline DICKERSON, b. 20 Dec 1849,
      Monticello, NY; d. 3 Dec 1897.

Children:
   + 695 M   i   Frank Livingston GROSVENOR, MD.
      696 F   ii   Mae Georgina GROSVENOR, b. 27 Jun 1882, Lebanon,
                   NY. She m. George Washington FINEN 5 Dec 1906.
                   George, son of Peter FINEN and Christine (____), b.
                   3 Aug 1884, Russia, NY.
                   Child: Helen.

542   John Payson GROSVENOR, b. 12 May 1877, Pomfret, Windham Co.,
      CT. He m. Helen BARROWS 14 Mar 1910. Helen, dau. of Harry
      BARROWS and Florence DAGGET, b. 23 Nov 1880, N. Attleboro, MA.

Children:
      697 M   i   Benjamin GROSVENOR, b. 27 Dec 1911, Pomfret,
                   Windham Co., CT.
      698 F   ii   Florence GROSVENOR, b. 24 Apr 1915, Pomfret,
                   Windham Co., CT.
      699 F   iii Constance GROSVENOR, b. 13 Sep 1917, Pomfret,
                   Windham Co., CT.

546   Walter James GROSVENOR, b. 4 Aug 1880, Pomfret, Windham Co.,
      CT; d. 6 Aug 1929, Boston, MA
           He m. Caro GRAYDON 2 Apr 1907. Caro, dau. of Alexander
      GRAYDON and Ada BAILEY, b. 16 Oct 1877, Malden, MA.

Children:
      700 F   i   Ada Miriam GROSVENOR, b. 29 Dec 1908, Cambridge,
                   MA. She m. Oliver Marble GALE Jr. 29 Aug 1931.

Oliver, son of Oliver GALE and Permelia NEWBY, b. 27 Jul 1908, Ventura, CA.

547 Thomas Hutchins GROSVENOR, b. 6 Mar 1886, Pomfret, Windham Co., CT.
     He m. Jessie KEENE 5 Jun 1917. Jessie, dau. of Frederick KEENE and Florence BROOKE, b. 22 Jan 1893, Dorchester, MA.

Children:
     701 M i   Thomas Hutchins GROSVENOR Jr. b. 25 Jan 1920, Forest Hills, MA.
     702 M ii Charles Richard GROSVENOR, b. 29 Apr 1925, Malden, MA.

549 Frank Alexander GROSVENOR, b. 6 Aug 1890, Pomfret, Windham Co., CT.
     He m. Helen Gertrude BATES 21 Feb 1914. Helen, dau. of Edgar BATES and Virginia SMITH, b. 16 Sep 1885, Trenton, NJ.

Children:
     703 F i   Elizabeth Scott GROSVENOR, b. 23 Oct 1915, Pomfret, Windham Co., CT.
     704 F ii Marguerite Bates GROSVENOR, b. 24 Aug 1917, Pomfret, Windham Co., CT.
     705 F iii Muriel Hutchins GROSVENOR, b. 21 Feb 1921, Pomfret, Windham Co., CT.
     706 F iv Arline GROSVENOR, b. 9 Jan 1923, Pomfret, Windham Co., CT.
     707 M v   Frank Leroy GROSVENOR, b. 8 Feb 1925, Pomfret, Windham Co., CT.

552 William GROSVENOR, b. 2 Nov 1886, Providence, RI. William was in W.W.1 as 2nd Lt. and Post Quartermaster. (Bowen)
     William GROSVENOR m. Mary BURNETT 16 Sep 1914. Mary, dau of Charles BURNETT and Ethel MASON, b. 21 Aug 1895, Peterboro, NH.

Children:
     708 F i   Mary Burnett GROSVENOR, b. 11 Jul 1915, Providence, RI.
     709 F ii Rosa Ann GROSVENOR, b. 22 Oct 1916, Providence, RI.
     710 F iii Caroline GROSVENOR, b. 29 Sep 1918, Providence, RI.
     711 M iv William GROSVENOR Jr. b. 7 Mar 1920, Providence, RI.
     712 M v   Charles Burnett GROSVENOR, b. Sep 1926, Providence, RI.
     713 M vi Richard GROSVENOR, b. Aug 1928, FRA.

556 Theodore Phinney GROSVENOR, b. 3 Jan 1897, Providence, RI.
     Theodore was a W.W.1 aviator on English Channel Patrol. (Bowen)

Theodore Phinney GROSVENOR m. Anita STRAWBRIDGE 14 Jun 1923. Anita, dau. of Robert STRAWBRIDGE and Anita BERWIND, b. 6 Jul 1902, PA.

Children:
```
714 F i    Anita GROSVENOR, b. 22 Apr 1924, Brookline, MA.
715 F ii   Pamela GROSVENOR, b. 18 Apr 1925, New York, NY.
716 F iii  Rose GROSVENOR, b. 1 Dec 1928, New York, NY.
```

EIGHTH GENERATION

571 Elmer Johnston GROSVENOR, b. 3 Oct 1891, Union City, IN; d. 11 Dec 1919.
Agriculturist, Manager of Grosvenor Farms. (Abbey Grosvenor)
     Elmer Johnston GROSVENOR m. Bertha May BROWN 26 Nov 1915. Bertha, dau. of Delmont BROWN and Clara PHILLIPS, b. 4 Dec 1894, Watertown, NY.

Child:
```
717 M i    David GROSVENOR, b. 6 Nov 1916.
```

573 Ivan Johnston GROSVENOR, b. 22 Dec 1897, Richmond, IN.
     Aviator in W.W.1. Michigan Auto School, Aero and Auto mechanic, Master Signal Electrician. Magazine writer and illustrator of Richmond, Indiana. (Abbey Grosvenor)
     Ivan Johnston GROSVENOR m. Florence Margaret BURGESS 25 Dec 1919. Florence, dau. of Lewis BURGESS and Minta BUNKER.

Child:
```
718 F i    Virginia Burgess GROSVENOR, b. 23 Jun 1922, Wayne
           Co., IN.
```

574 Richard Browne GROSVENOR, b. 29 Apr 1916, Columbus, Franklin Co., OH.
     Richard graduated from Kent State U. with a B.Sc. in Ed. in 1938. He is a retired high school history teacher with hobbies of bird watching, walking, swimming and genealogy.
     Richard Browne GROSVENOR m. Anna May HAWLEY 13 May 1943, Warren, Trumbull Co., OH. Anna, dau. of Miller Henry HAWLEY and Carrie Ethel DEVOR, b. 21 Feb 1917, Malta, Phillips Co., MT; c. 10 Sep 1922, United Brethren, Malta, Phillips Co., MT. Dick and Anna are retired and live at Vida, OR.
     Anna is a retired secretary and now is doing a lot of volunteer work. Scheduling for the Vida-McKenzie Neighborhood Watch is done by her. As a result of this scheduling she has been trying to promote a Thirteen Month Calendar to start with the year 2000. Each month to have four equal weeks. That's 364 days. That extra day will not have a number but will be a special holiday. The Year 2000 will be Leap Year and it will be celebrated at the end of the year (again without a number). So to begin the new millenium we can start it off with a grand celebration of two special holidays.

She volunteers at the Oregon Genealogical Society preparing the members' Pedigrees for publication in the Quarterly, also on the Book Repair Committee in their library twice a month. Her computer is busy each month recording the finances of the McKenzie Valley Presbyterian Church.

She worked in the Mortgage Loan Office of the Prudential Insurance Company of America in Phoenix AZ for twelve years and retired in 1972. Then she kept and cared for her senile Mother for six years.

She was employed in the office of the Registrar of Contractors in the state of Arizona from 1955 to 1959. Prior to her marriage she wound stators for electric motors at the Sunlight Electric Co. (later General Motors) in Warren OH from 1935 to 1943.

At the age of 18 she was bedridden for about six months as the result of a burst appendix. Many prayers and a Visiting Nurse were her healing blessings.

Children:
+   719 F i   Dorothy Jean Grosvenor.
    720 F ii   Susan Mae GROSVENOR, b. 19 Apr 1950, Warren, Trumbull Co., OH.

Born in Ohio, Susan was raised in the Arizona desert where the family enjoyed lots of traveling, camping and exploring of Indian ruins. She began taking piano lessons at the age of seven and later studied violin, cello and other musical instuments. Susan was awarded an honor in the Phoenix Symphony Guild Concerto Competition. While majoring in music at Arizona State University, she had a spiritual out-of-body experience that changed her life and led to an innovative music healing technique later in life. She discontinued her formal music education.

She and her first husband hitchhiked from Arizona to New Hampshire before starting their first music group. Later they went on the road, doing shows in Oregon, Washington and on Kodiak Island in Alaska.

At age 31 Susan realized that she naturally heard musical tones when focusing her attention on people and other aspects of life. This led to work as a composer for short films, videos, theatre and radio productions. While in Oregon, she taught piano, released an album of piano compositions and participated on a CD of various artists. The music that she improvised for people was therapeutic. She called the therapeutic work Personal Alchemical Music.

She met Paul SPEARS when he studied piano with her. They married in a private ceremony on Christmas Eve 1989. They had a second ceremony in the summer of 1990 beside the McKenzie River at the

Presbyterian Church at Leaburg OR and invited all
friends and relatives. They moved to Arizona where
Paul worked at the Arizona Sonora Desert Museum.
Susan played organ in a local church and continued
with her music work.

Susan enjoys treks in nature. She has no
children, although she had an orange cat named Fred
who was a close friend for twenty years.

Susan Mae GROSVENOR m. (1) James "Jim" Findley
KENNEDY Jr. 12 Dec 1971, Phoenix, Maricopa Co., AZ;
they divorced. James, b. 5 Nov 1949. He received
a degree in Psychology from Arizona University at
Tucson and a doctorate in Research Psychology from
the University of North Carolina.

She m. (2) Paul Douglas SPEARS 24 Dec 1989,
Portland, OR. Paul, son of Douglas Duane SPEERS
and Alice CHAPMAN, b. 11 Jan 1965, Seattle, King
Co., WA.

Paul received his B.S. in Geography in 1989
from the University of Oregon. He is the Assistant
Purchasing Agent at the Arizona Sonora Desert
Museum. He spent time at the Planetarium as a
Guide and has composed soundtracks for the
Planetarium shows at OMSI in Eugene, OR.

575   Florence Olive GROSVENOR, b. 12 Feb 1918, Columbus, Franklin
Co., OH; d. 12 Dec 1977, Los Angeles, CA.

Florence was an outstanding music student in school. She
played piano for the orchestra in high school and excelled in
music at Kent State Unviersity from which she graduated in
1940. She taught school for awhile but did not like it. When
she married Bob ORPIN in 1942, they moved to New York City
where he played the piano and sang in night clubs. Florence
taught piano lessons at home and played the organ in church.
They had one child, Robert, who shares his parents' musical
talents.

Bob died in Texas in 1955. Florence continued her work
in New York. She later married again but the marriage soon
ended in divorce. In 1966 she started caring for her mother.
She bought a new home so her mother could have a bedroom on
the first floor. After five years Mother went to a nursing
home in Canada and Florence soon moved to Los Angeles. She
bought an apartment house and rented the apartments. She
continued to play the organ in church.

In 1975 she developed cancer of the throat. She had
smoked since her college days. She had chemotherapy and
surgery and died in 1977. In accordance with her instructions
her ashes were scattered on the grounds of the crematorium.
(RBG)

Florence Olive GROSVENOR m. (1) Robert "Bob" ORPIN May
1942. Robert, b. 7 Mar 1918; d. 1955, TX.

Bob majored in music and graduated from Kent State
University in 1940. He played the piano and sang at Night

75

Clubs. While touring with the band in Texas, he slipped in a bath tub that had no bath mat and was drowned. (RBG)

Child:
+   721 M i   Robert Grosvenor "Robin" ORPIN.

576   Jean Frances GROSVENOR, b. 7 Jun 1920, Columbus, Franklin Co., OH. Jean intended to be a physician but her father was laid up with a heart attack and no scholarships were available. She took elementary education and graduated with a BS in Ed at Ohio State U. in 1941. (She married Joe Berger in June 1941.) She took graduate work but because of Joe's numerous transfers she did not qualify for her Master's Degree.

  She taught at Spokane, WA from 1942 to the spring of 1944 when Joe was transferred by the Air Force from Spokane. In 1952 she started teaching again intermittently while Joe was in the Service. She taught at the AF Dependents' School at Ramstein, Germany from 1953 to 1955. On their return to the United States she taught at Wakarusa, IN and Belleville, IL, then at Millstadt from 1958 to 1963. In 1963 they went to Japan and she taught at a private school for one year, and then taught English to engineers at Mitsubushi. Upon their return to the United States she taught 5th grade in Bend, OR until her retirement in 1978. She found teaching very interesting and enjoyed it.

  Jean's main hobby was travel. She had plenty of this as Joe was stationed many places in the West and Midwest during WWII. While they were stationed in Ramstein, Germany, they took weekend jaunts to Holland, France, and Italy. These trips were their chief form of recreation. While living in Japan she visited Korea, Okinawa, Taiwan, Siam and India. Her trip through central India included the Taj Mahal and many other interesting sites. However she was upset by the extreme poverty of India and the difference between the rich and the poor. Later she visited Singapore and Malaysia and was amazed at the high energy and industry of the people. A visit to Hong Kong showed a people working hard to become modern.

  Jean Frances GROSVENOR m. Joseph Herman "Joe" BERGER, DVM 19 Jun 1941, Christ Church, St. Louis, MO. Joseph, son of Emil F. BERGER and Rosa ROSTI, b. 4 Nov 1913, Madison Twp., St. Joseph Co., IN; c. 21 Jun 1914, Zion United, Madison Twp., St. Joseph Co., IN.

  When Joe was 16 his doctor examined him for a severe loss of energy and a very rapid heart beat. He was informed that he had an acute rheumatic fever infection brought on by strep infected tonsils. His doctor arranged to assist a specialist who would remove his tonsils. On the day of his surgery Joe drove the Model T, unaccompanied, to the specialist's office in Mishawaka, IN where his tonsils were removed under local anesthetic. He then drove home and followed his normal week of chores and school except for drinking warm milk instead of eating as his throat was sore and swallowing was painful.

He returned to the doctor to have the stitches removed and was advised that without complete bed rest he might not survive the next six months. If he did survive, his physical activities would have to be severely limited and he could expect to live perhaps 30 or 40 years. This was normal for such situations at that time. This grim news motivated him to train himself to make a living at other than farming.

Joe graduated from Madison High School in 1934 and took a year of pre-veterinarian school at Purdue. He graduated from the Ohio State College of Veterinarian Medicine in 1939. Upon graduation he went to work for the Health Commissioner of the City of St. Louis in the area of Milk Control. The city was the first major metropolitan area to adopt and enforce the U.S. Public Health Service Standard Milk Ordinance and Code. The two years that he spent at St. Louis were the highlight of his training for his major life's work.

Upon graduation from Ohio State U. Joe had been commissioned a First Lt. in the Veterinary Corp Reserve and had been placed on active duty for six weeks at Carlisle Barracks, PA.

Early in 1940 Joe joined the Second Air Force Headquarters at Spokane, WA as a Veterinarian. He was assigned both Public Health and Food Inspection duties in the Army Air Corps.

Throughout WWII and subsequently, he was, at every assignment, responsible for all aspects of preventative medicine except immunization and venereal disease control. He finished his wartime service at Colorado Springs and left the Service with the rank of Major in the Spring of 1946.

When he left the Service, Joe practiced Veterinary Medicine at Nyssa, OR, a pioneering Mormon area on the Snake River. In 1948, Joe returned to the U.S. Army Air Corp with the rank of Major. He served at Carswell Air Force Base, Fort Worth, TX and then at the Surgeons Office at Omaha. At this time the U.S. Army Air Force was redesignated the U.S. Air Force.

In 1950 he was selected to attend the Harvard University School of Public Health. Upon graduation in 1951 (with his Master's Degree) he was assigned to the 5th Air Force HQ in Weisbaden, Germany. After a four year tour he was assigned to the Military Headquarters Transport Service (MATS) at Andrews Field, Washington, D.C. MATS installations covered the globe and frequent travel to all of these was routine. Early in 1958 he was promoted to full Colonel. After five years at MATS he was transferred to Japan where he visited Air Force installations in Japan, Okinawa, Korea, Taiwan, Philippines, Thailand and Vietnam. Upon completion of his three year tour he was sent to Wright Patterson Air Force Base, Dayton, OH where he was discharged at his retirement in October 1966.

On retirement Joe took his family to Bend, OR where he worked for the Department of Agriculture as Assistant State Veterinarian for Disease Control. He was responsible for Deschutes, Jefferson, Lake, Wheeler and Crook Counties.

This was a most delightful area and a very satisfying experience. After 12 years he retired on his 65th birthday.

Joe's hobbies included travel which was part of every job and photography that was useful for preparation of staff reports and recreation. He enjoyed planting trees, shrubs and flowers at each new housing location while in the service and still follows this hobby in retirement.

An auto accident in 1980 severely brain damaged Jean. A task of rehabilitation was undertaken that will continue for the rest of her life. They have received greatly appreciated help from family and friends. An optometrist has restored her eyesight almost to its original condition. Quadraped cycles were built for both Jean and Joe and Jean's use of the cycle has restored most of her balance and given her enjoyment.

In 1985 Jean and Joe took a six week train trip in Europe. In 1987 they took a six week camping trip in their VW Van to Alaska, British Columbia, the Yukon and Kodiak Island. Since 1993 Jean and Joe have been going to Sun City, AZ, in the winter where Jean enjoys ideal weather and cycling conditions.

Children:
+   722 M i   James Dennis BERGER.
+   723 M ii   Jack Edwin BERGER, MD.
+   724 M iii Jerry Reid BERGER.
+   725 F iv   Jeanetta Sue "Susie" BERGER.
+   726 M v   Jesse Frederick BERGER.

577 Theodore Park "Ted" GROSVENOR, Ph.D, b. 19 Apr 1923, Cuyahoga Falls, Summit Co., OH.

Ted is an Optometrist, optometric educator, and author of optometric textbooks. Ted received his B.Sc. in Optometry from Ohio State University in 1946 and his Ph.D. in optics from Ohio State University in 1956.

His interests are music, camping, hiking, travel, and writing. He migrated with his family to Auckland, New Zealand (1964-1969) and to Canada (1970-1974), then returned to the United States. He currently is retired in rural southern Indiana.

Theodore Park GROSVENOR m. Elizabeth Eleanor DAVIS May 1945. Elizabeth, dau. of Charles Raymond "Pop" DAVIS and Florence WORTHING, b. 4 Mar 1926, Worthington, Franklin Co., OH.

Her occupations are homemaker, teacher (elementary), volunteer in adult education unit (G.E.D.). She is retired from the work force at present.

She attended Ohio State University, University of Houston and University of Auckland, New Zealand. She received her Teaching Certificate at Auckland Teachers College, Auckland, New Zealand in 1966. She took a course in Computer Repair at Houston, Texas in 1984. Her hobbies are camping, hiking, writing, music, teaching adults to read, teaching life skills and travel.

Children:
+   727 M i   Frederick David "Fred" GROSVENOR.
     728 F ii   Barbara Jean GROSVENOR, b. 4 Sep 1950, Franklin,
                 OH. Barbara is a computer operator in Seattle, WA.
     729 M iii James Edward GROSVENOR, b. 30 Nov 1954, Columbus,
                 Franklin Co., OH.
                      James is leader of the "Fat James," band at
                 Seattle, WA.

578 Charles George GROSVENOR, b. 6 Dec 1872, Piqua, OH; d. 13 Jul
     1913. He m. (1) Laura Belle FOSNAUGH 10 Sep 1895. Laura,
     dau. of Simon FOSNAUGH and Julia CLEVIDENCE, b. 1 Aug 1876,
     Fairfield Co., OH; d. 7 Jul 1904.

Child:
+   730 M i   McKinley Hobart GROSVENOR.

     Charles m. (2) Susan Rose FRIEHOFER 24 Jun 1907. Susan, dau.
     of Solomon FRIEHOFER and Matilda ROBINS, b. 10 Feb 1885,
     Piqua, OH; d. 30 Jun 1932.

Children:
     731 F ii   Grace Louise GROSVENOR, b. 10 Feb 1911, Piqua, OH.
     732 M iii Charles Walter GROSVENOR, b. 1 Jan 1913, Piqua, OH.

582 Earl Willis GROSVENOR, b. 13 Feb 1880, Piqua, OH.
     He m. Elsie Marie BIXLER 23 Jun 1909. Elsie, dau. of Eli
     BIXLER and Ann ETTER, b. 20 Feb 1893, Piqua, OH.

Child:
     733 F i   Florence Augusta GROSVENOR, b. 25 Apr 1910.

585 Vernon Myers GROSVENOR, b. 30 Dec 1886, Piqua, OH.
     He m. Viola Myrtle WHITEHURST 5 May 1914. Viola, dau of Luke
     WHITEHURST and Margaret ORANGE, b. 20 Feb 1893, Widewater, VA.

Children:
     734 M i   Walter Vernon GROSVENOR, b. 28 Jul 1915, Glen
                Allen, VA.
     735 F ii   Margaret Lillian GROSVENOR, b. 8 Jun 1917, Piqua.
                OH.
     736 M iii John Pershing GROSVENOR, b. 2 Dec 1918, Piqua, OH.
     737 M iv   Donald Richard GROSVENOR, b. 20 Jul 1926, Piqua,
                OH.
     738 M v   Clarke Edward GROSVENOR, b. 9 May 1928, Piqua, OH.

597 George Benton GROSVENOR, b. 1 Sep 1861, Dubuque, IA; d. 1 Jul
     1932. He m. Jessie Caldwell LYON 10 Oct 1883. Jessie, dau.

of Delos LYON and Cecilia HOWARD, b. 3 Jun 1861, Dubuque, IA; d. May 1916.

Children:

739 M i   Graham Bethune GROSVENOR, b. 22 Jul 1884, New York, NY; d. 28 Oct 1943.

Graham started as a mechanic with the Otis Elevator Company in 1902 and became Vice President and Western Manager at San Francisco. He became a special assistant to the President of Pan American Airways and played an outstanding part in the rise of America's network of airlines. At one time he was President of the Aviation Corporation and Vice President of Fairchild Aviation Corporation. (Who's Who)

Graham Bethune GROSVENOR m. Mary RITCHIE 28 Feb 1910. Mary, dau. of John RITCHIE and Minnie EVERSON, b. 22 Dec 1888, Syracuse, NY.

+   740 M ii   George Howard GROSVENOR.

602 Gilbert Hovey GROSVENOR, b. 28 Oct 1875, Constantinople, Turkey; d. 4 Feb 1966.

Gilbert Hovey GROSVENOR attended Amherst where he and his brother Edwin were one of the best tennis doubles teams. He graduated in 1897 and taught two years at Englewood Academy. He joined the National Geographic Magazine at the invitation of Graham BELL. He began as Assistant Editor and only full time employee of the small and irregularly published technical journal. The company soon transferred its headquarters to New York City where the magazine would be on newsstands. Gilbert opposed this and when printing costs soared and circulation stood still the headquarters was moved back to Washington.

In 1900 he married Elsie BELL, the daughter of Alexander Graham BELL, and became Managing Editor. He became Editor-in-Chief in 1903.

He introduced an unprecedented amount of photography into the magazine and started color photography in 1910. He took the pictures himself or bought them from government agencies. Members of his editorial committee opposed his use of pictures. In January 1911 he found eleven vacant pages that must be filled immediately. He filled them with pictures of Lhasa, Tibet with captions only and expected to be fired. The response was so favorable that he was elected to the company's Board of Managers.

He published non-technical articles on wildlife, travel and exploration. He sold memberships to the society instead of subscriptions and secured tax exemption as a non-profit educational organization. He used magazine revenues for scientific research projects such as polar explorations and archeological digs. He encouraged explorers Peary, Byrd and Amundsen and his map of Antarctica was used by Admiral Byrd. The National Geographic photographic library became one of the largest and most valuable in the world.

Under his leadership the membership of the society increased from 900 to 1,250,000. He became president of the society in 1920 and Chairman of the Board of Trustees in 1954. Gilbert wrote many books and magazine articles and served as a trustee of George Washington and American Universities of Washington, DC. He served as Chairman of the Board of the National Geographic Magazine until his death in 1966. (National Geographic Magazine, Oct 1966)

Gilbert Hovey GROSVENOR m. Elsie May BELL 23 Oct 1900, London, EN. Elsie, dau. of Alexander Graham BELL and Mabel HUBBARD, b. 8 May 1878, London, EN.

Children:
+   741 M i   Melville Bell GROSVENOR.
      742 F ii   Gertrude Hubbard GROSVENOR, b. 28 Jul 1903.
                  She m. Paxton BLAIR 5 Dec 1925. Paxton, son of
                  Joseph BLAIR and Eugenie KRUTTSCHNITT, b. 30 Sep
                  1892, New Orleans, LA.
                  Children: Joan and Edwin.
      743 F iii   Mable GROSVENOR, b. 28 Jul 1905; d. 1933.
      744 F iv   Lillian Waters GROSVENOR, b. 8 Apr 1907.
                  She m. Cabot COVILLE 28 Jul 1927. Cabot, son of
                  Frederick COVILLE and Elizabeth BOYNTON.
                  Children: Gilbert and Cabot.
      745 M v   Alexander Graham Bell GROSVENOR, b. 9 Jul 1909,
                  Washington, DC; d. 5 Mar 1915.
      746 F vi   Elsie Carolyn Alexander GROSVENOR, b. 3 Mar 1911,
                  Washington, DC.
      747 F vii   Gloria GROSVENOR, b. 17 Sep 1918, Bethesda, MD.

603   Edwin Prescott GROSVENOR, b. 28 Oct 1875, Constantinople,
      Turkey; d. 28 Feb 1930, N.Y. City, NY
          Edwin Prescott GROSVENOR was born in Turkey and attended
      Roberts College at Constantinople until his family came to the
      United States. He graduated from Amherst College in 1897 and
      taught several years at Chestnut Hill Academy of Philadelphia.
      He entered Columbia Law School in 1900 and graduated in 1903.
      He worked for the Federal Government on enforcement of anti-
      trust and interstate commerce laws. He prosecuted the
      "tobacco trust" and won the only criminal conviction against
      the notorious "night riders" who terrorized the tobacco
      growing area of Kentucky.
          After 1914 he joined the New York law firm of Cadwalder
      Wickersham and Taft where he developed a large practice. He
      was also general counsel for the National Geographic Society
      and for other large corporations. When the United States
      entered World War I he served under the chief of staff of the
      intelligence division. He was a Republican and a
      Congregationalist. (Cyclopedia Vol 21)
          Edwin Prescott GROSVENOR m. Thelma SOMERVILLE 26 Oct
      1918.

Children:
        748 F i   Anne Somerville GROSVENOR, b. 5 Aug 1919, New York,
                    NY.
        749 F ii   Louise Taft GROSVENOR, b. 25 Jul 1921, York Harbor,
                    ME.

604   Asa Waters GROSVENOR, b. 7 Nov 1874, Constantinople, Turkey.
       He m. Gertrude King HANNA 27 Oct 1904. Gertrude, dau. of
       Oliver HANNA and Mary NUTTMAN, b. 3 Oct 1881, Ft. Wayne, IN.

Children:
        750 F i   Julia Hanna GROSVENOR, b. 4 Aug 1905, New Castle,
                    PA.
        751 M ii   Jonathan Holman GROSVENOR, b. 30 Jan 1907,
                    Flushing, NY; d. 17 Jan 1909.
        752 F iii Florence Waters GROSVENOR, b. 6 Dec 1912, Ft Wayne,
                    IN.

612   Leonard Arthur St. John GROSVENOR, b. 13 Oct 1881, Montcalm,
       MI; d. 21 Jul 1957, Los Angeles, CA.
       Leonard's mother labeled him "hard to take care of" and sent
       him to live with an Aunt. He learned farming from her husband
       (Alonzo Kennedy) and enlisted in the army as Arthur Grosvenor
       in 1901. He served three years in the Philippines. After his
       service he married Mary Teller in Detroit where he worked as
       a street car conductor. They moved to South Dakota where he
       trapped wolves and coyotes on an Indian Reservation. They
       then homesteaded in Wyoming but this was a hard life and they
       returned East where he worked on the railroad. He died in a
       Veterans Hospital. (Jeanette Grosvenor)
            Leonard Arthur St. John GROSVENOR m. Mary Louise TELLER
       31 Mar 1908, Detroit, MI. Mary, b. 19 Jul 1887.

Children:
+   753 M i   Herbert Leroy GROSVENOR.
        754 F ii   June Viola GROSVENOR, b. 21 Jul 1910, Detroit, MI;
                    d. 7 Dec 1969, Anaheim, CA.
                    June did not marry. She stayed with her father
                    until his death and then lived with her sister
                    Dolores. (Jeanette Grosvenor)
        755 M iii Leonard Arthur GROSVENOR Jr., b. 18 Jan 1912,
                    Teton, SD. Leonard was a telegrapher. He handled
                    his father's farm during the depression and went to
                    Montana in 1945 and worked on a ranch. He then
                    went back to telegraphing for the railroad. He
                    traveled much and did not marry. (Jeanette
                    Grosvenor)
        756 F iv   Erma Evelyn GROSVENOR.
        757 M v   Carroll GROSVENOR.
        758 M vi   Robert Marion GROSVENOR.
        759 F vii Alice Louise GROSVENOR.
        760F viii Lola Delores GROSVENOR

616 George Tracy GROSVENOR, b. 5 Aug 1893, Wilcox Twp., Newaygo
     Co., MI; d. 26 Jun 1960, Traverse City, MI.
          George moved with his parents and sisters to North
     Manitou Island in 1909. He was ready for high school but the
     local school had only eight grades. His parents and the
     parents of another boy each paid the teacher $10 a month to
     teach high school subjects. George worked for a lumber mill
     for seven years and then began carrying the mail between
     Leland and Manitou Island. He carried the mail in a boat
     across Lake Michigan to the Island except in winter when he
     walked across the ice, a walk of as much as 32 miles a day.
     In summer he carried the cherry pickers to the island and
     brought back the crop.
          George married Della FIRESTONE and they alternated their
     residence between Leland and Manitou Island. Their three
     children were born while they lived on the Island. For two
     years George served as Leland Township Treasurer. In 1952
     George retired from mail delivery and became manager of the
     Island. It was owned almost entirely by the North Manitou
     Island Association. George and Della retired from the job in
     1957 and moved to Leland. They were members of the Immanuel
     Lutheran Church in Leland. (Jeanette Grosvenor)
          George Tracy GROSVENOR m. Della B. FIRESTONE 15 May 1918,
     Suttons Bay, MI. Della, dau. of Albert FIRESTONE and Marie
     NERLAND, b. 29 Jul 1895, North Manitou, Leelanau Co., MI; d.
     5 May 1972, Northport, Leelanau Co., MI.

Children:
     761 F i   Shirley GROSVENOR, b. 24 Sep 1913, Leland, MI.
                She m. Otto George SWARZ Jr. 11 Sep 1939. Otto,
                son of Otto George SWARZ and Weds PACPE, b. 24 Mar
                1918.
                Children: Tracy and Thomas.
     762 F ii   Fern GROSVENOR, b. 29 Oct 1924, Leland, MI; d. 24
                Sep 1965, Leland, MI.
                She m. Harry GARTH 14 Dec 1944. Harry, b. 17 Aug
                1922.
  + 763 M iii George Firestone GROSVENOR.

619 Ralph Collins GROSVENOR, b. 1 May 1895, Claridon, Geauga Co.,
     OH; d. 6 Apr 1966, Claridon, Geauga Co., OH.
          Ralph graduated from high school in 1912 as a member of
     a class of three. He served in the Marine Corps in W.W.1. He
     was in the fifth generation to farm his township home and was
     chosen "Farmer of The Year" by the Northern Ohio Farmers Club
     in 1955. When asked for the reason for his success he
     modestly attributed it to good rock removal, with dynamite if
     necessary. He was a seventh degree Granger and served as
     Master. He served on the School Board and was a Trustee of
     the Township and the Claridon Congregational Church.
     (Jeanette Grosvenor)
          Ralph Collins GROSVENOR m. Belle SAMPSON 25 Oct 1920.
     Belle, dau of Elbert Alonzo SAMPSON and Eva Zerviah BATTLES,

EIGHTH GENERATION

b. 5 Sep 1897, McGraw, Warren Co., PA; d. 11 Oct 1962, Claridon, Geauga Co., OH.
     Belle was active as a member of the Congregational Church and as a volunteer in the Community Hospital. She was a seventh degree Granger and served as Secretary for twenty years. (Jeanette Grosvenor)

Children:
    764 F i   June Adeline GROSVENOR, b. 22 Aug 1921, Claridon, Geauga Co., OH.
               She m. Charles Cotton KELLOGG 23 Aug 1941. Charles, son of Frank KELLOGG and Della SCHUTE, b. 2 Apr 1914, Geauga Co., OH.
               Children: Dennis and Harold.
    765 F ii   Ruth Jeanette GROSVENOR, b. 2 Feb 1924, Claridon, Geauga Co., OH.
               Jeanette was a SPAR with the Coast Guard for two years during World War Two. She has a Bachelor of Science Degree from A and M College in Stillwater, Oklahoma and is a teacher with hobbies of carpentry and genealogy. She is the Compiler, Editor and Publisher of "The Descendants of Nathan E. Grosvenor and Laura Fuller 1794-1973."
               Ruth Jeanette GROSVENOR m. (1) James William MAIDEN 26 Jan 1943, Chester, Hancock Co., W. Va. James, b. 23 May 1920.
               She m. (2) Alfred CHRISTOFERSON 10 Sep 1949, Stillwater, Payne Co., OK; they divorced.
    766 M iii Ralph GROSVENOR Jr. b. 6 Dec 1929, Chardon, Geauga Co., OH.
               Ralph served three years in the Air Force. He graduated from Ohio State University with DVM Degree in 1959. He is a member of the Elks and Kiwanis. (Jeanette Grosvenor)
               Ralph GROSVENOR Jr. m. Janet Elaine MIRACLE Jul 2, 1954, Mechanicsburg, Champaign, Co., OH. Janet, dau. of Virgil MIRACLE and Florence ASHER, b. 29 Dec 1929, Columbus, Franklin Co., OH.
    767 F iv   Janice GROSVENOR, b. 14 Feb 1937, Chardon, Geauga Co., OH. She m. Frank STANEK, Chardon, Geauga Co., OH. Frank, son of James STANEK and Valeria BOGDNASKI, b. 3 May 1937, Cleveland, OH.

633 Millard GROSVENOR, b. 1853; d. 1923. He m. (1) Ellen OTTMAN. Ellen, b. abt 1852.

Child:
    768 F i   Blanche GROSVENOR.

Millard GROSVENOR m. (2) Martha SAFFORD. Martha, b. 1865; d. 1932.

EIGHTH GENERATION

641   Arthur GROSVENOR, b. 14 Apr 1866; d. 21 Jul 1946.
          He m. Susan KNISKERN 1891. Susan, b. 24 Oct 1871; d. 2
       Jun 1929.

Children:
       769 M i   Stillman GROSVENOR, b. 5 Jul 1893; d. 1896.
       770 F ii   Mae GROSVENOR, b. 12 Jul 1897; d. 17 May 1976.
                  She m. Ray SMITH 1920. Ray, b. 17 Jun 1898.

644   Sidney GROSVENOR, b. 2 Aug 1874. He m. (1) Lillian WINDSOR.

Child:
       771 F i   Marion GROSVENOR.

       Sidney m. (2) Adele SUMMERS.

655   Verner Calvin GROSVENOR, b. 3 Mar 1879, Grosvenor Corners, NY;
       d. 20 Dec 1943.
       He m. (1) Sarah Gladys GUFFIN Nov 1904. Sarah, b. 6 Oct 1885;
       d. 10 Mar 1906.
       He m. (2) Alice BOUCK 6 Jun 1912. Alice, dau. of Hamilton
       Becker BOUCK and Emily VAN KLEEK, b. 6 Aug 1879; d. 13 Jun
       1961.

Child:
       772 M i   John Henry GROSVENOR, b. 9 Jun 1913. He m. Marion
                  MCCAUL 1939.

658   Ernest GROSVENOR, b. 18 Jun 1892; d. 31 Dec 1929.
          He m. Lillian CHISLET 6 Apr 1912. Lillian, dau. of James
       CHISLET and Lettie (_____), b. 2 Nov 1892.

Children:
+   773 M i   James GROSVENOR
       774 F ii   Virginia C. GROSVENOR, b. 7 May 1916. She m. (1)
                  Arthur John LOHNER 29 Sep 1916. Arthur, b. 18 Aug
                  1913; d. 9 Oct 1946.
                  She m. (2) Edward KOBISCHEN 25 Jun 1955.
       775 F iii Henrietta GROSVENOR, b. 1 Oct 1917. She m. Chester
                  Edward SMITH 23 Oct 1949.
                  Child: Mark Dean.
       776 F iv   Dorothy J. GROSVENOR, b. 22 May 1928. She m.
                  Maurice P. HALE, Jr. 15 Jun 1951.

661   Willis Lee GROSVENOR, b. 5 Nov 1909.
          He m. Ann Elizabeth FRIDER 25 Apr 1942. Ann, dau. of
       Charles Dewitt FRIDER and Elizabeth Catherine KENNEDY, b. 18
       Jan 1905.

Children:
       777 M i   David GROSVENOR, b. 16 Jun 1943.
       778 M ii   Kent GROSVENOR, b. 7 Aug 1947. He m. Cheryl
                  PRESTON 1 Jun 1968.

EIGHTH GENERATION

779 F iii Elizabeth Ann GROSVENOR, b. 19 Apr 1950. She m. Terry PALMER 4 Aug 1973.

666 Girdeon Parley GROSVENOR Jr, b. 11 Nov 1882, Council Bluffs, IA. He m. Bessie PLUMMER.

Children:
      780 M i   Jack Girdeon Parley GROSVENOR, b. 9 Jun 1918, Council Bluffs, IA.
      781 M ii   Theodore Russell GROSVENOR, b. 14 Jul 1921, Council Bluffs, IA.
      782 M iii Gordon Dee GROSVENOR, b. 13 Sep 1926, Council Bluffs, IA.

678 Julius GROSVENOR, b. 1886. He m. Gussie COYLE.

Children:
      783 F i   Dorothy GROSVENOR m. (____) LAMBERSON.
      784 F ii   Hattie GROSVENOR m. Ross KLEFFAN.
      785 M iii Carl GROSVENOR.
      786 M iv   Delbert GROSVENOR m. Elba HOWARD.

682 Homer Douglas GROSVENOR. He m. Marie SMITH.

Children:
      787 F i   Emma GROSVENOR.
      788 F ii   Nellie GROSVENOR.
      789 F iii Helen GROSVENOR.
      790 M iv   Frank GROSVENOR.

683 Thomas GROSVENOR, b. abt 1900. He m. Elenor BROWNING.

Children:
      791 F i   Ada GROSVENOR.
      792 F ii   Betty GROSVENOR.
      793 F iii Marcine GROSVENOR.

695 Frank Livingston GROSVENOR, MD, b. 15 Jul 1875, Lebanon, NY; d. 14 Oct 1945, Hartford, CT
      Frank Livingston obtained his MD at the U. of Buffalo in 1900. He was head of the Medical Department of Travelers Insurance Co. directing the work of 20,000 doctors until his retirement in 1945. He was a Presbyterian and a Republican. (Cyclopedia, Vol 40)
      Frank Livingston GROSVENOR, MD m. Helen ALLEN 1 Jun 1904. Helen, dau. of John ALLEN and Helen MCCAUL.

Children:
      794 M i   Allan Livingston GROSVENOR, b. 31 Jul 1908, Hartford, CT; d. 31 Jan 1931.
      795 F ii   Nancy Mackin GROSVENOR, b. 8 Dec 1921, Hartford, CT.

719   Dorothy Jean GROSVENOR, b. 18 Jul 1945, Warren, Trumbull Co., OH. She graduated in 1963 with honors in secretarial courses and journalism from Sunnyslope High School in Phoenix, AZ. She immediately began a career in the legal field, first as legal secretary and later as a paralegal. She was a member of and pursued her continuing education through Pacific Northwest Legal Assistants.
       After 30 years in law, she left it to pursue other interests, including a longtime love of travel and gardening. She studied French and business at Lane Community College in Eugene, OR. She is a graduate of an international tour management institute. She and Norm traveled often in Europe, and teach a class at the local community college on travel in France.
       Dorothy Jean GROSVENOR m. (1) Jack Lee WILLIAMS 18 Jul 1963, Phoenix, Maricopa Co., AZ; they divorced. Jack, son of Alfred WILLIAMS (twin) and Edna Lee CANEER, b. 23 Nov 1940, E. St. Louis, IL.

Child:
+   796 F i   Renee Yvonne WILLIAMS.

       Dorothy m. (2) Stanley Loren HALL 25 Aug 1972; they divorced. Dorothy m. (3) Norman CHOLEWINSKI 30 Aug 1988, Eugene, Lane Co., OR. Norman, son of Edward CHOLEWINSKI and Hazel May RUCKER, b. 6 Mar 1956.
       Norm obtained his B.S.E.E. from Oregon State University in 1981. Since 1988 he has been a sole proprietor consulting in the areas of instrumentation and rehabilitation engineering under the name of Performance Data Systems. Other interests include photography, running, music, and international travel. He and Dorothy are restoring their country property in Springfield, OR.

721   Robert Grosvenor "Robin" ORPIN, b. 13 Nov 1946, Jackson Heights, NY. Robert is a City Planner at Long Beach, CA.
       He m. Claudia (____). Claudia, b. 22 May 1946.

Children:
       797 M i   Robert Joshua ORPIN, b. 9 Jan 1970.
       798 F ii   Maggie Grosvenor ORPIN, b. 18 Oct 1975.

722   James Dennis BERGER, Ph.D. b. 16 Jul 1942, Spokane, Spokane Co., WA. James is head of the Department of Zoology at the University of British Columbia at Vancouver, Canada.
       James earned his degrees in Zoology at Indiana University, Bloomington, IN. He received his A.B. in 1964 with distinction, his A.M. in 1965 and his Ph.D. in 1969. He was Assistant Professor at British Columbia U. 1970 to 1975, Associate Professor 1976-1992 and has been Professor since 1992. He was Director of the Biology Program 1991-1996 and has been head of the Department of Zoology since 1996. His

interests are research and teaching of cell biology and genetics.

He is a member of Gloria Dei Lutheran Church. North Vancouver, British Columbia.

James m. Gail Eileen PATTON 27 Mar 1967 at Bloomington, IN. Gail was b. 14 Sep 1944 at Evansville, IN and is the daughter of Daniel PATTON and Dorothy GREEN.

The University of Indiana awarded Gail her AB in English with distinction in 1966 and her AM in English in 1970. She is an instructor in English at Douglas College at New Westminster, B.C. and teaches rhetoric and literature. She serves on the Bargaining Team of the Douglas College Faculty Association.

Children:
    799 M i   Joel BERGER, b. 16 Aug 1972, Bloomington, IN.
    800 M ii Justin BERGER, b. Apr 1981, Vancouver, B.C., CAN.

723 Jack Edwin BERGER, MD, b. 5 Oct 1944, Boise, ID. Jack is a Physician at Davis, CA.

He received his A.B. in Zoology at Indiana University in 1966, and his M.D. at Washington University School of Medicine in 1971. His Residency was completed in Family Practice at Kaiser Permanente Hospitals in Los Angeles in 1975. He was certified as Diplomate of the American Board of Family Practice in 1975, 1982, 1988 and 1995.

He was beaten by Chicago police at the Democratic National Convention in 1968. He has a hobby of bicycling and in 1996 had two bike accidents with three fractures and two broken helmets.

Jack m. (1) Doris SHOCKLY Jun 1966, Bloomington, IN; they divorced. Doris b. 6 Nov 1943 in IN.

Children:
    801 M i   Christopher BERGER, b. 4 Jul 1970, St. Louis, MO.
    802 M ii Joshua BERGER, b. 26 Jun 1974, Los Angeles, CA.

Jack m. (2) Tonya Lee HILLIS, b. 31 Jul 1943 in Los Angeles, CA. Tonya is the daughter of Donald Roy HILLIS, and Florence HAMILTON. She has a B.S. in Environmental Design from U.C. at Davis, CA (1977). She enjoys gardening, basil farming and sheep husbandry. She raises and trains Australian Shepherds.

724 Jerry Reid BERGER, b. 1 Jan 1949, Ft. Worth, TX. Jerry earned his AB in Zoology at Indiana U. in 1970. He is the owner of Autopia, an automobile service business, in Eugene, OR. He owned two other businesses previously.

Jerry m. (1) Kimberly Ann YORK 5 Oct 1975, Seattle, WA.

Children:
    803 F i   Amariah Cleona BERGER, b. 8 May 1974, Seattle, WA.
    804 M ii Kalin BERGER, b. 15 Jun 1977, Eugene, Lane Co., OR.

Jerry m. (2) Martha "Marti" AMBERGER 6 Nov 1985, Sky Camp Lodge, Lowell, Lane Co., OR; they divorced.

Child:
805 F iii Clair BERGER, b. 21 Jun 1991, Eugene, Lane Co., OR.

Jerry m. (3) Heather Lynn MCCONNELL Sep 1995.
    Heather was born in Troy, Ohio. She is the daughter of Glen Gorrell MCCONNELL and Betty Frances PHILLIPS. She earned her B.A. at Ohio State U. in 1972 and a B.A. from Eastern Oregon in 1978. She works at computer sales and marketing.

725 Jeanetta Sue "Susie" BERGER, b. 6 Jul 1950, Omaha, Douglas Co., NE. Susie is an office worker in Eugene, Oregon.
    Susie m. Michael JACKSON.

Children:
806 M i   Michael David JACKSON-BERGER, b. 31 Dec 1978, Washington, D.C.
807 M ii   Gabriel James JACKSON-BERGER, b. 8 Feb 1981, Virginia Beach, VA.
808 M iii Jason Edward JACKSON-BERGER, b. 15 Oct 1984, Virginia Beach, VA.
809 F iv   Tina Louise JACKSON-BERGER, b. 16 Feb 1987, Virginia Beach, VA.
810 F v   Clarissa Jean JACKSON-BERGER, b. 21 Feb 1990, Eugene, Lane Co., OR.

726 Jesse Fredrick BERGER, b. 6 Jul 1956, Mishawaka, St. Joseph Co., IN.
    Jesse is an Automotive Technician and business owner of "Fat City" a firm specializing in the repair of German automobiles. He started "Fat City" at Seattle, Washington, at the age of 16 with his brother Jerry. Jesse left the business for several years to work as a carpenter/contractor and as a marine engineer on fishing boats. His later work took him to Alaska in 1980. In 1982 he reopened "Fat City" and in 1995 purchased his present Seattle building which houses his auto repair business and his wife's law office.
    Jesse lived in Tokyo, Japan, as a child (1963-1966) and then moved to Bend, Oregon. He left home in 1972 and lived for a year with his brother Jack and Jack's wife in Pasadena, California. He then moved to Seattle and bought his present home. He met Carol EDWARD in California and married her in 1982. While they were on their honeymoon in Indiana they helped Grandpa Emil BERGER celebrate his 100th Birthday.
    Jesse m. Carol EDWARD 5 Jun 1982, Walnut Creek, Contra Costa, CA. Carol was born at Lewiston, ID on 24 Nov 1957.
    Carol is an Immigration Attorney, a wife, mother and business partner.

Children:
811 M i   Joey BERGER.

812 M ii Zephyr BERGER.
813 M iii Griffin BERGER, b. Jun 1994.

727 Frederick David "Fred" GROSVENOR, b. 21 Apr 1949, Dayton, OH.
Fred has a BA in psychology from Aukland, NZ. He has had
various computer courses since then. He has worked as a
Computer Programmer Analyst since 1985. He was formerly a
Production Planner/Scheduler for seven years.
     His main interest is music. He has a large collection
and plays a guitar.
     Fred m. Cathie Theresa HARDING, NZ; they divorced.
Cathie, dau. of Peter Martin HARDING and Margaret Theresa
CLEARY, b. 21 Oct 1952, Kawakawa, Northern Dist, NZ.

Children:
+   814 M i   Benjamin Nicholas "Ben" GROSVENOR.
     815 F ii Sara Jean GROSVENOR, b. 2 Jun 1977, Otahuhu,
                Auckland, NZ.

730 McKinley Hobart GROSVENOR, b. 16 Oct 1896, Piqua, OH.
     He m. Cecil Jane ROWE 24 Dec 1917. Cecil, dau. of Isaac
ROWE and Mary LEONARD, b. 13 Aug 1891, Champaign Co., OH.

Children:
     816 M i   Roger Nigel GROSVENOR, b. 7 Nov 1925, Urbana, OH.
     817 F ii Mary Jane GROSVENOR, b. 21 Jan 1927, Columbus,
                Franklin, OH.
     818 M iii William Howard GROSVENOR, b. 22 Aug 1930, Columbus,
                Franklin, OH.

740 George Howard GROSVENOR, b. 18 Apr 1888. He married.

Children:
     819 M i   Howard Lyon GROSVENOR
     820 F ii Elizabeth GROSVENOR m. George Walton SEARLES.

741 Melville Bell GROSVENOR, b. 26 Nov 1901, Washington, DC; d. 22
     Apr 1982.
          Melville graduated from the Naval Academy in 1923 and
     served on the battleship Connecticut as a midshipman. He
     sailed 18,000 miles through tropical waters shoveling coal
     into fire boxes. In 1924 he completed his service with the
     Navy and joined the National Geographic Magazine as an
     Assistant Editor.
          Melville served a 33 year apprenticeship before becoming
     Editor and President. In the early days the budget was tight
     and he used his own money to travel to Europe. He made
     photographs with glass plates and wrote articles. He was a
     pioneer in color photography taking pictures from a dirigible.
     He loved traveling in his yawl 'White Mist' and wrote about
     his travels.
          As Editor he was always trying new ideas. He published
     the first National Geographic Atlas of The World, an instant

success. He created the first map globe that spun on its axis. He signed Jacques Cousteau to give lectures and write articles that made him famous. He backed Dr. Leakey's research in Africa that made him known. Melville created the Society's first television series, a winner of eight Emmy Awards. When he retired in 1977 the National Geographic Society was the largest educational organization in the world.

After retiring he headed the National Park Service Advisory Board and campaigned to create the Redwood National Park. (National Geographic Magazine, Aug 1982)

Melville Bell GROSVENOR m. Helen North ROWLAND 4 Jan 1924. Helen, dau. of Herbert ROWLAND and Susie NORTH, b. 21 Dec 1902, Waterbury, CT.

Children:
    821 F i   Helen Rowland GROSVENOR, b. 24 Dec 1925, Washington, DC.
    822 M ii   Alexander Graham Bell GROSVENOR, b. 24 Dec 1925, Washington, DC.
+   823 M iii Gilbert Melville GROSVENOR.
    824 F iv   Sara Ann GROSVENOR.

753 Herbert Leroy GROSVENOR, b. 25 Jan 1909, Detroit, MI; d. 13 Oct 1953, Stockbridge, MI.
    He m. Edna FISHER 9 Apr 1939. Edna, dau. of Charles FISHER and Jane LOAR, b. 2 Jan 1918.

Children:
+   825 M i   Edward Arthur GROSVENOR.
+   826 M ii   Carroll Leroy GROSVENOR.

763 George Firestone GROSVENOR, b. 16 Oct 1921, Leland, MI.
    George operated the mail boat to Leland.
    He m. Florabelle Louise SCHECK 6 Feb 1946. Florabelle, dau. of Albert SCHECK and Stella HARWOOD, b. 19 May 1922, Masich, MI.

Children:
    827 F i   Constance Lou GROSVENOR, b. 7 Jan 1947, Traverse City, MI.
               She m. James Frederick NIESSINK 1 Oct 1966. James, b. 4 Jul 1946, Detroit, MI.
               Child: Geoffrey.
+   828 M ii   George Michael GROSVENOR.

773 James GROSVENOR, b. 11 Apr 1913. He m. Ruth Marion STEWART 12 Apr 1936.

Child:
    829 F i   Donna Lou GROSVENOR, b. 10 Dec 1946. She m. Douglas MCCRINDLE 2 Mar 1968.

796 Renee Yvonne WILLIAMS, b. 6 May 1964, Phoenix, Maricopa Co., AZ; c. Jan 1965, Cross Roads Methodist Church, Phoenix, Maricopa Co., AZ.

Renee attended Marist High School in Eugene, OR and earned an A.A. at Lane Commuity College. She briefly attended the University of Oregon and continued her education at Lane C.C., becoming a licensed massage therapist. She pursues international travel and photography.

Renee m. Craig Randall SORSETH 9 Apr 1994, Sweet Home, Linn Co., OR. Craig, son of Alvin Lloyd "Tyke" SORSETH and Arlene Joyce SPORTSMAN, b. 6 May 1947, Sweet Home, Linn Co., OR.

Craig earned a B.S. in political science and an M.S. in Public Administration at the University of Oregon and works for the state of Oregon. He and Renee, with their son Noah, live on the property homesteaded by his grandparents in Sweet Home, OR.

Child:
830 M. i Noah Nakai SORSETH, b. 12 Aug 1996, Sweet Home, Linn Co., OR.

814 Benjamin Nicholas "Ben" GROSVENOR, b. 10 May 1973, Otahuhu, Auckland, NZ.

Ben worked at fast food places until September 1993 when he joined the Navy. Ben is stationed at the Great Lakes Naval Training Station where they serve 15,000 men per meal. He is a cook supervisor and has supervised as many as 300 cooks. He orders supplies and maintains inventories.

Ben attended school in New Zealand and Cincinnati, OH. He plans to go to college on the GI Bill as soon as his Navy enlistment is completed. He enjoys automobiles, having had eighteen cars in seven years.

Ben m. Lora Nicole "Nikki" MORLEY 15 Feb 1992. Nikki was born 5 March 1972 at Franklin, IN. She is employed in a retail store and hopes to go to college after Ben completes his education.

Child:
831 M i Brendan GROSVENOR, b. 23 Nov 1992, Bloomington, IN.

823 Gilbert Melville GROSVENOR, b. 5 May 1931, Washington, DC.

Gilbert graduated from Yale and joined the National Geographic in 1954. He has served as Editor since 1970. (Who's Who)

Gilbert Melville GROSVENOR m. Donna C. KERHAM 6 Jun 1961.

Child:
832 M i Gilbert Harvey GROSVENOR

825 Edward Arthur GROSVENOR, b. 25 Apr 1942, Woodland, MI.

He m. Jonnie LIPKE 30 Jul 1966, Lincoln Park, Wayne Co., MI. Jonnie, b. 17 Aug 1947 Detroit, MI.

Children:
        833 M   i   Edward Arthur GROSVENOR Jr. b. 14 Jul 1967.
        834 M   ii   Kevin Peter GROSVENOR, b. 26 Mar 1969, Pontiac, MI.
        835 M   iii Charles Herbert GROSVENOR, b. 30 Mar 1971, Pontiac,
                     MI.

826   Carroll Leroy GROSVENOR b. 18 Dec 1943, Wise Twp., MI.
          Carroll served in the army 1965-1967. Six months of his
      service was in Vietnam. He is an employee of Pontiac Motors.
          He m. Lorraine BUGBEE 13 Jan 1968, Flint, MI. Lorraine,
      b. 4 Jan 1943, Mt. Morriss,
Children:
        836 M   i   Stephen GROSVENOR, b. 15 May 1964, Flint, MI.
        837 M   ii   John Carroll GROSVENOR, b. 18 Nov 1968, Pontiac,
                     MI.
        838 M   iii Eric Leroy GROSVENOR, b. 22 Jan 1970, Lapeer, MI.
        839 F   iv   Crystal Lee GROSVENOR, b. 1 Dec 1971, Lapeer, MI.

828   George Michael GROSVENOR, b. 7 Jan 1947, Traverse City, MI.
          He m. Elizabeth HAMMACK 28 Jun 1968. Elizabeth, dau. of
      Ben HAMMACK and Arlena SMITH, b. 15 Nov 1940, Tecumseh, MI.

Children:
        840 M   i   George GROSVENOR, b. 29 Nov 1970, Grand Rapids, MI.
        841 F   ii   Molly GROSVENOR.
        842 F   iii Mary Ann GROSVENOR.
        843 M   iv   David Albert GROSVENOR, b. 13 Dec 1983, Traverse
                     City, MI.
        844 F   v   Sarah GROSVENOR.

SOURCES

ANCESTRY & DESCENDANTS OF JOHN GROSVENOR OF ROXBURY, MA

PUBLISHED SOURCES

New England Historical and Genealogical Register, 1918, Vol 72. "English Home and Ancestry of John Grosvenor of Roxbury, MA." by Daniel Kent. (Kent)

"The History of Woodstock, Connecticut," Vol. # 6, by Clarence Winthrop Bowen, Ph.D., LL.D., 1935. Privately Printed. (Bowen)

"Descendants of Nathan E. Grosvenor and Laura Fuller, 1794-1975" by Miss Jeanette Grosvenor. Privately Printed. (Jeanette)

Who's Who in America" published by Marquis Who's Who, A Reed Reference Publisheing Co. (Who's Who)

"Burke's American Families of English Ancestry, 1939" by the Genealogical Publishing Co. (Burke's)

NATIONAL GEOGRAPHIC MAGAZINE by the National Geographic Society.

"Biographical Directory of the Congress of the United States, 1774-1988, 1989" published by the U.S. Government Printing Office.

"The National Cyclopedia of American Biography, 1895-1984" published by James T. White and Co. 1985. (Cyclopedia)

"History of Miami County, Ohio, 1880" by W. H. Beers.

"The War of the Rebellion" by Chauncey F. Grosvenor, Published by Heritage Inc., 1994.

The History of Shropshire" Victorian Series, Vol III.

OTHER SOURCES

"Grosvenor Pedigree" Manuscript by Abbey Grosvenor, 1923. (Abbey Grosvenor)

"The Grosvenors of Schoherie and Montgomerie Counties, N.W." Manuscript by Lindsley Reese Bailey, 1977. (Bailey)

Letter from Suzanne Soltess on 22 November 1966. (Suzanne Soltess)

Autobiographies received from descendants of John Grosvenor.

Town Records of Fairfax, Vermont.

(The names in parentheses following each source
is used in the text to identify the source.)

DOCUMENTS IPO RICHARD GROSVENOR

Pages from a Grosvenor Family Bible, includes records of births, deaths and marriages from 1755 to 1923.

DANIEL GROSVENOR DOCUMENTS
        Statement for Bounty Land, 1818.
        Certificate of Masons membership, 1818.
        Admittance to the Ohio Bar, 1822.
        Masons Resolutions upon the death of Daniel Grosvenor, 1867.

CHAUNCEY GROSVENOR DOCUMENTS
        Discharge from the 147th Regiment, O.V.I., 1864.
        Discharge from 17th Regiment, O.V.I., 1865.
        Marriage Certificate of Chauncey and Florence Locke, 1871.
        "Red Snapper Fishing" by Chauncey Grosvenor, 1893.
        U.S. Army and Navy Association History of Chauncey, 1900.
        Tribute to Chauncey Grosvenor from the G.A.R., 1902.

FRED BROWNE GROSVENOR DOCUMENTS
        Troy High School Graduation Speech, 1904.
        Troy High School Commencement Program, 1904.
        Ohio State University Commencement Program, 1908.
        Michigan University Commencement Program, 1911.
        Ohio Certificate to Practice Medicine, 1911.
        Certificate of Masons' membership, 1918.
        Certificate: 1st Lieutenant in the Army Reserve Corps, 1918.
        Certificate of promotion to Captain, 1919.
        Wartime Diary, 1918-1919.

SISTERS OF FRED BROWNE GROSVENOR - DOCUMENTS
        Troy High School Diploma, Clifford, 1894.
        Troy High School Commencement Program, Clifford, 1894.
        Troy Normal School Diploma, Clifford, 1895.
        Troy High School Commencement Progra, Frances, 1895.
        Troy High School Commencement Program, Corinne, 1897.
        Ohio Life School Certificate, Clifford, 1923.
        D.A.R. Membership Certificate, Corinne, 1941.
        Will of Clifford Grosvenor, 1954.

www.ingramcontent.com/pod-product-compliance
Lightning Source LLC
Chambersburg PA
CBHW082359270326
41935CB00013B/1691